SOUL PORTRAITZ

Created, Written, and Illustrated by Taurean Washington

All Characters are under copyright and trademark and solely for owner of the mark and intellectual property of Taurean Washington

All rights reserved.

No part of this book may be reproduced or used in any manner without the prior written permission of the copyright and trademark owner.

To request permissions, contact the publisher Taurean Washington at
ceo@cr8nst8n.com

Amazon Paperback ISBN: 9798343240795

Cover by: Taurean Washington

Illustrated by: Taurean Washington

Copyright 2024

CR8N ST8N LLC

www.cr8nstin.com

Frederick, MD, 21701

Cr8n St8n LLC

owned by entrepreneur Taurean Washington, Cr8n St8n LLC has it's own original intellectual property but also has done amazing designs for the following :

NBA

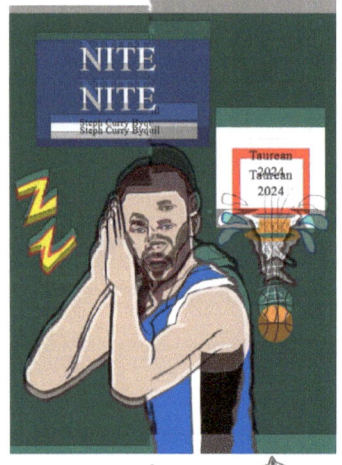

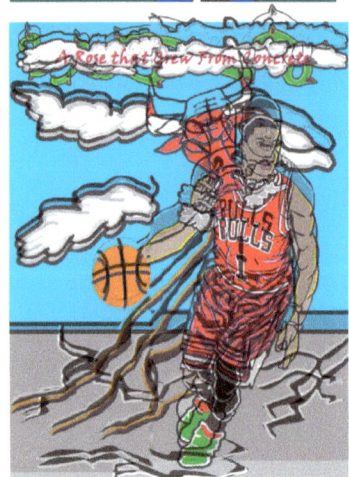

WNBA

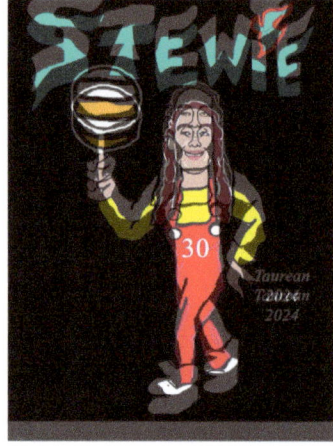

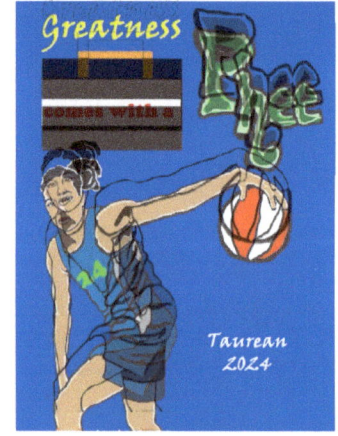

DISNEY

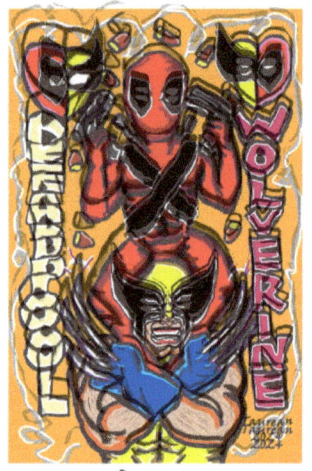

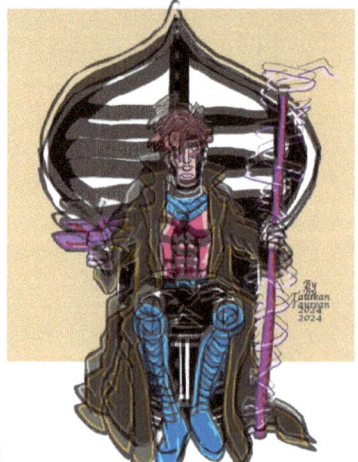

visit us here (QR CODE)

We put paint where it aint!

This Book is Dedicated to Dr. Opal Lee aka "The Grandmother of Juneteenth"

Thank you for your courage, loving heart, and tenacity!

You are an inspiration!

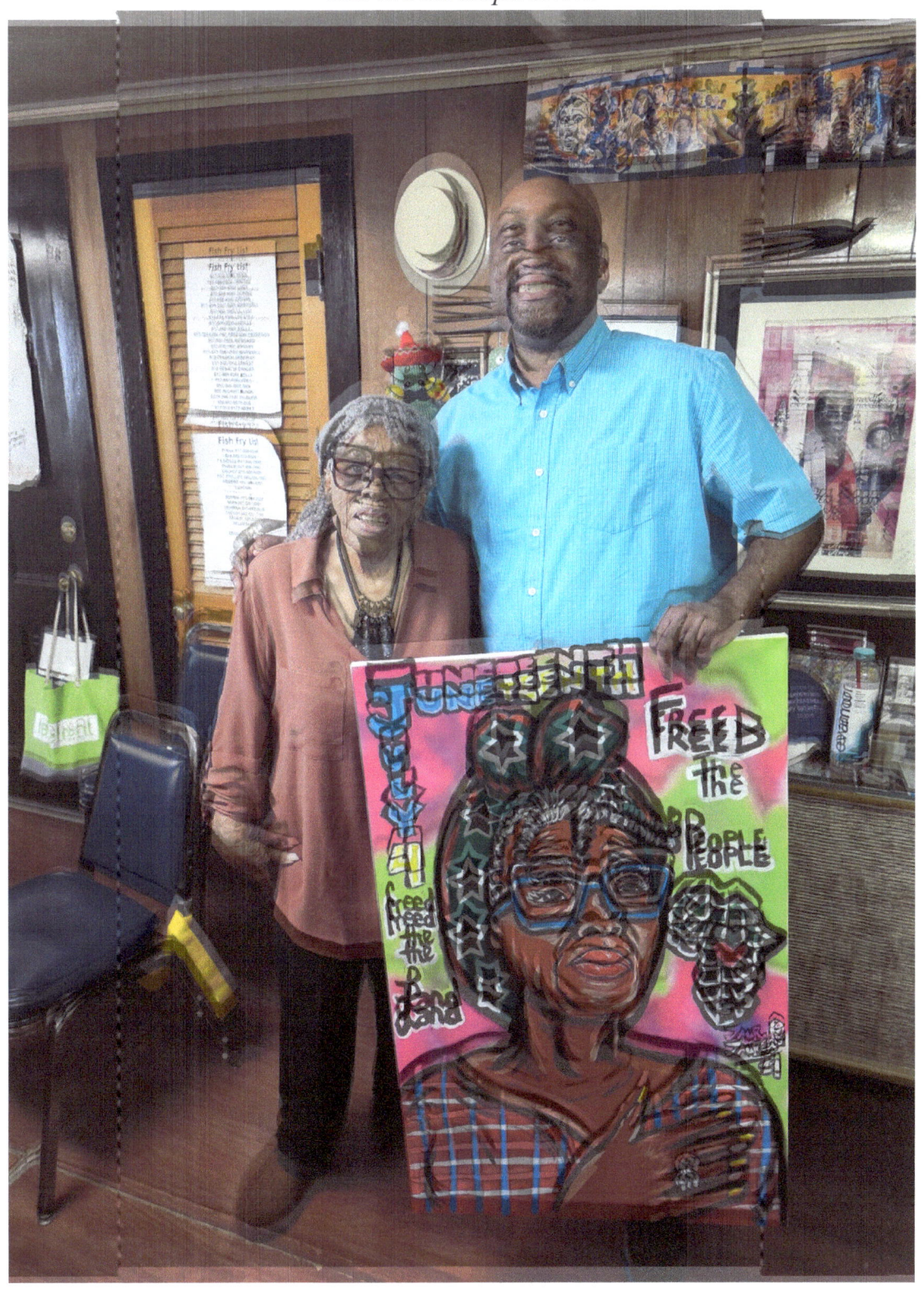

FOREWARD

Portraits have always been something I've been captivated by. Realism has not been something I have ever been focused on until recently and I want to work on that component to my game.

But if I've ever done portraits, I always wanted to capture the Soul of someone and have different elements to the piece to describe the person I'm depicting.

My goal is to separate myself as an artist in all facets and I have seen many over the years do portraits of hip-hop musicians and public figures and I always wanted to find a way to do something different.

This collection of works are items I've done as early as 2008.

I want to show you my full bag including my showcase of drawing with charcoal. I took about a 10-year break from drawing around 2013 and just got back into drawing in 2023 so from 2024 and beyond, I'll keep working on my drawing game and take that to the next level.

I hope you enjoy the images displayed. My goal is to lay my imprint down and give you something special with each person I depict.

Enjoy!

Taurean Washington

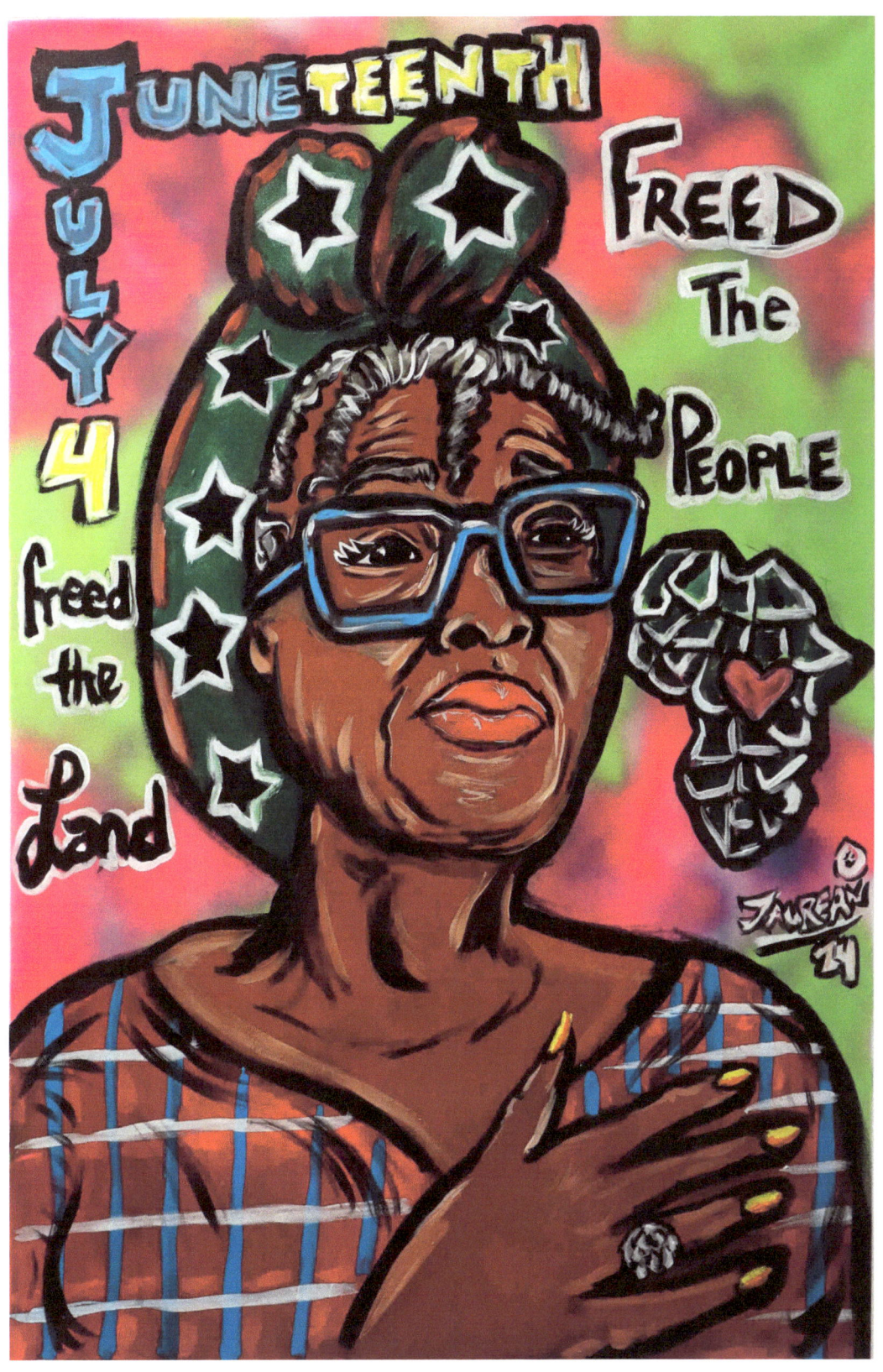

Dr. Opal Lee (2024)

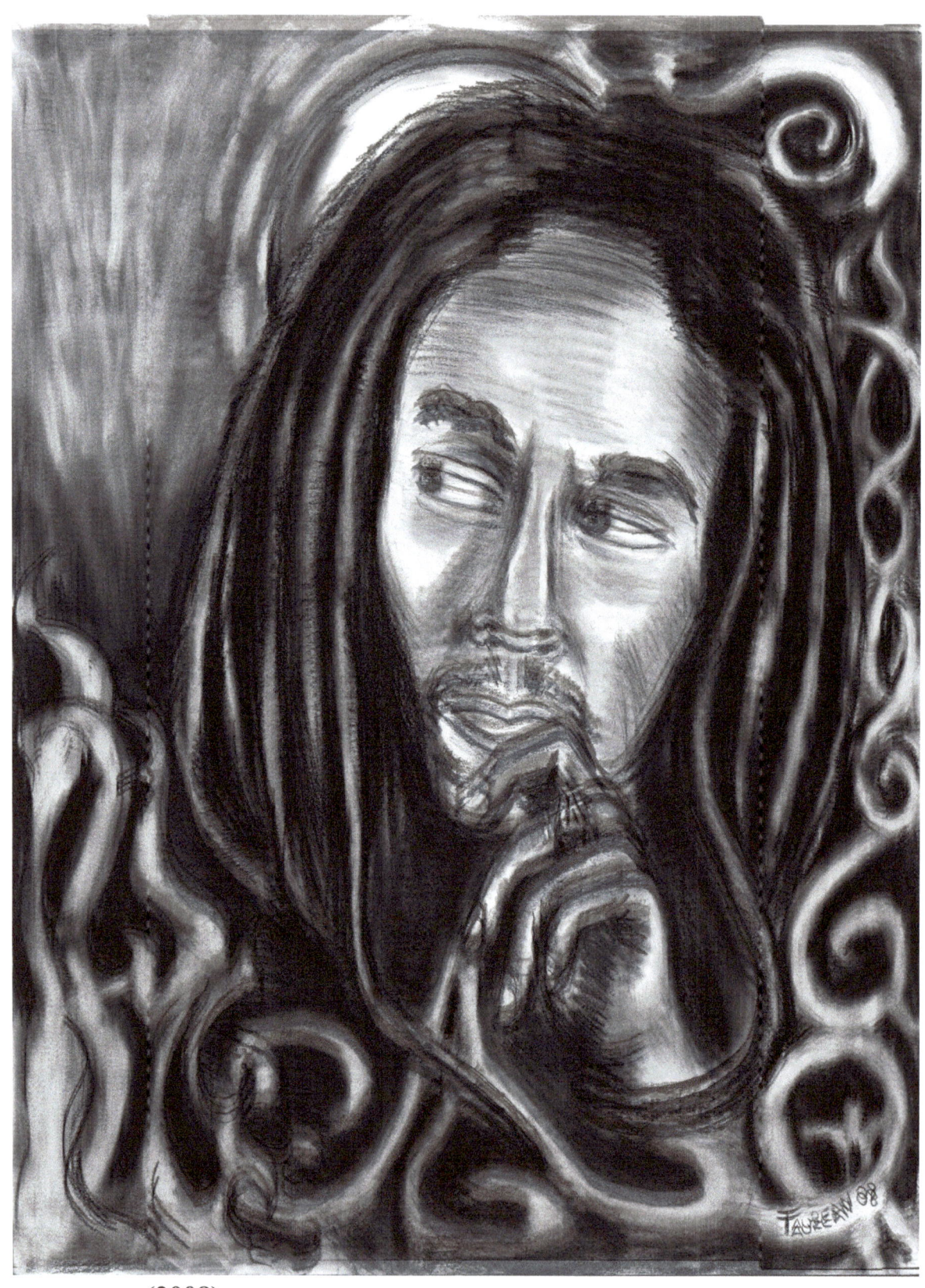

Bob Marley (2008) Rest in Peace

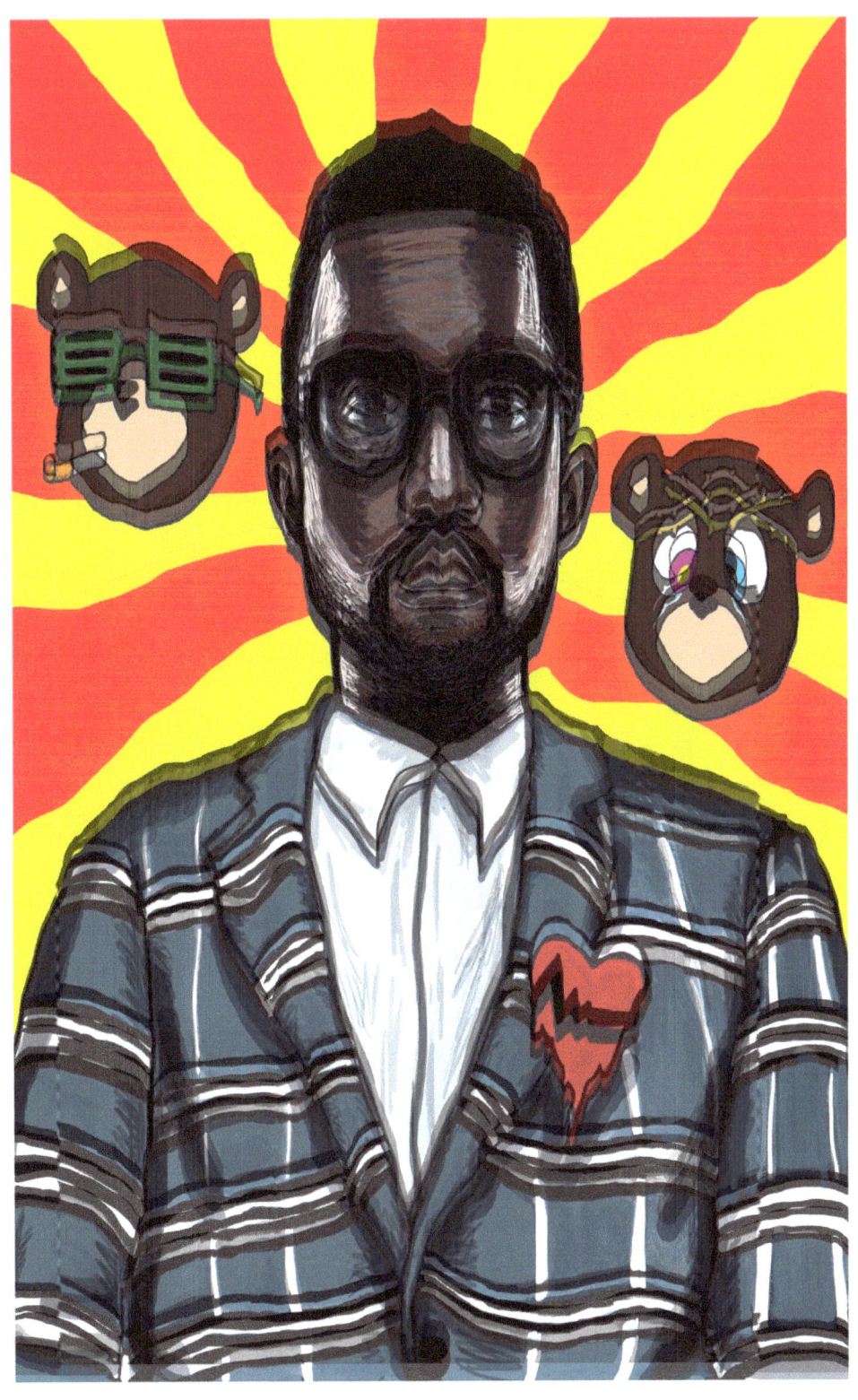

Kanye West (2016)

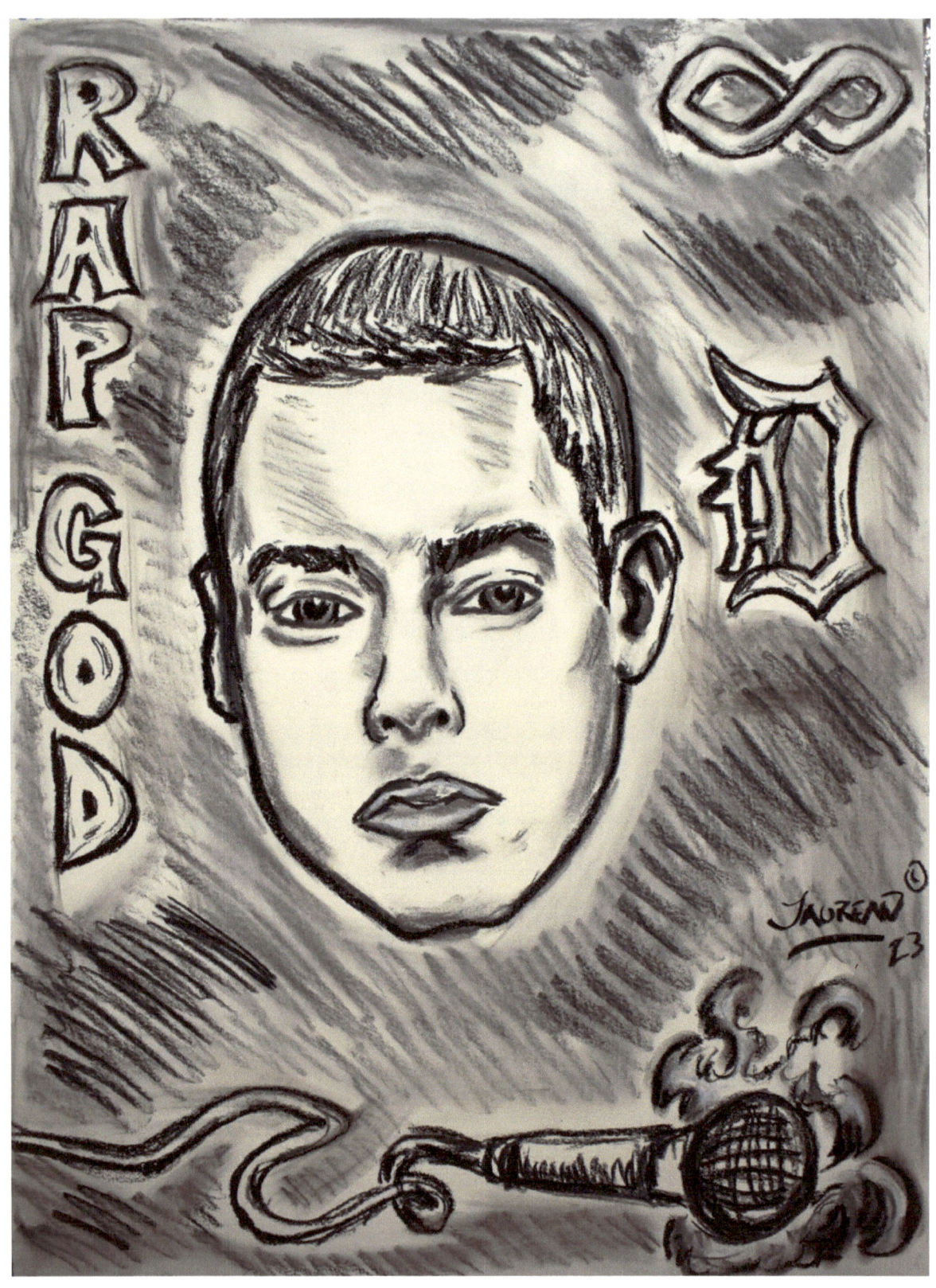

Eminem (2023)

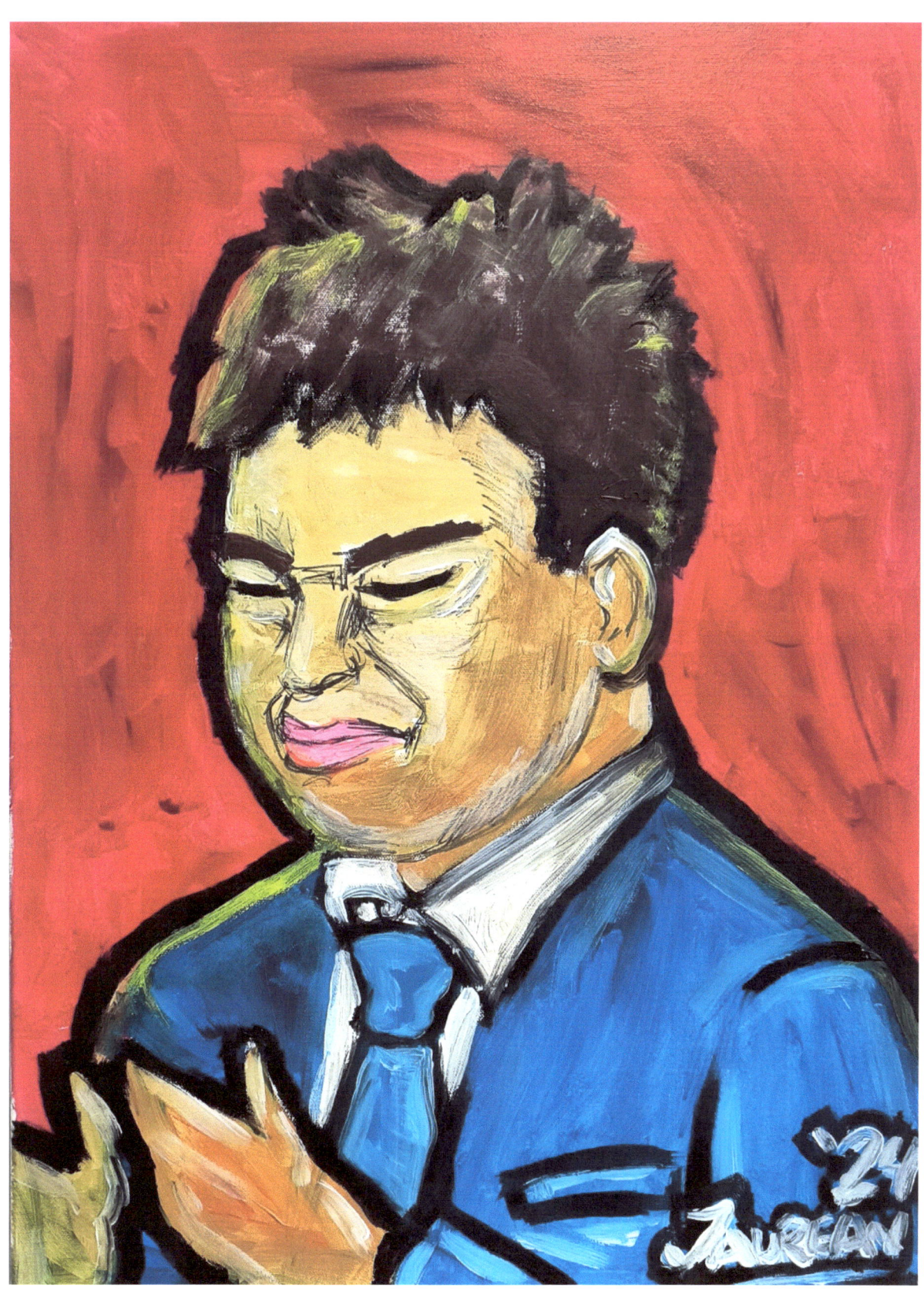

Gus Walz (2024)

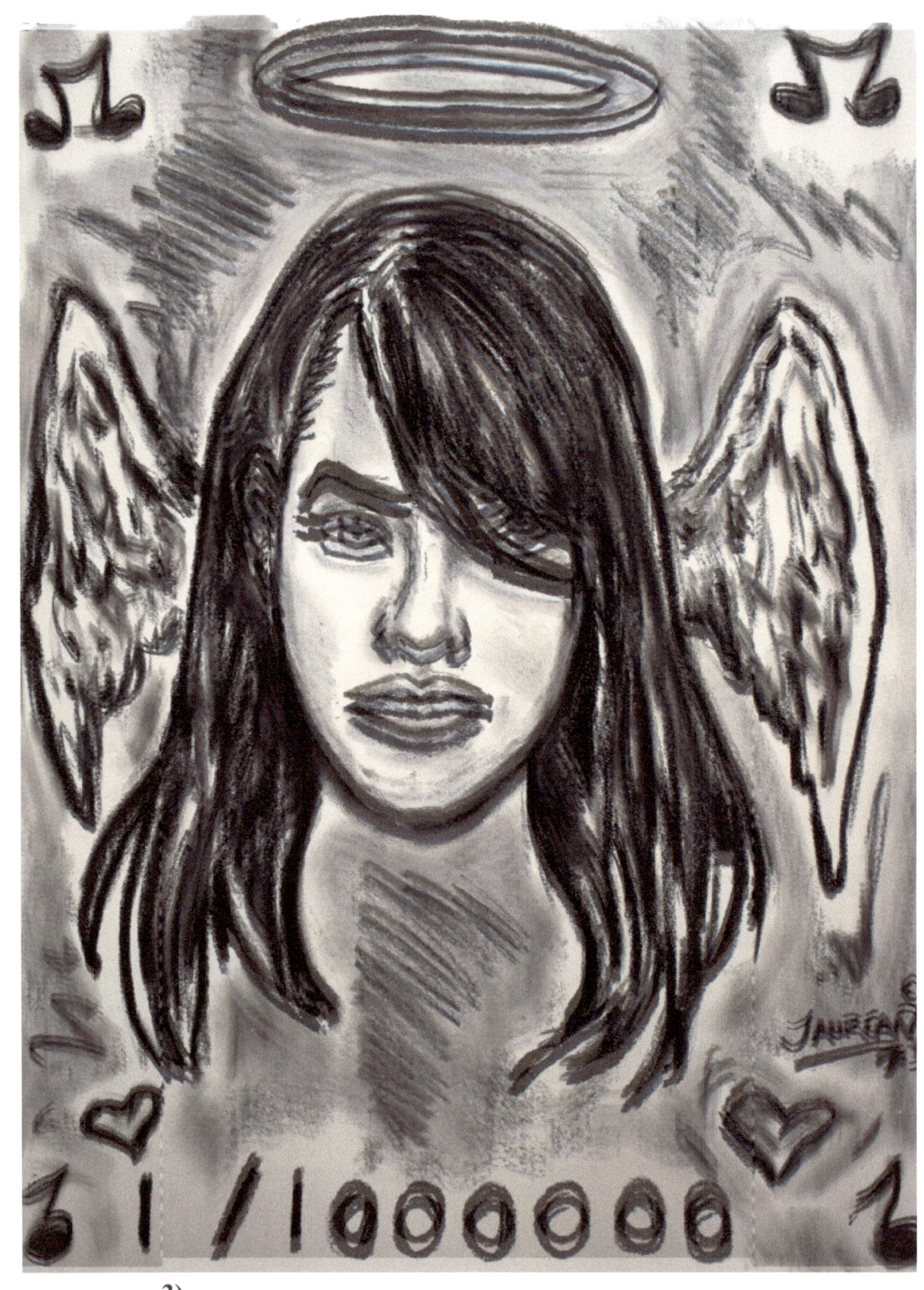

Aaliyah (2023) Rest in Peace

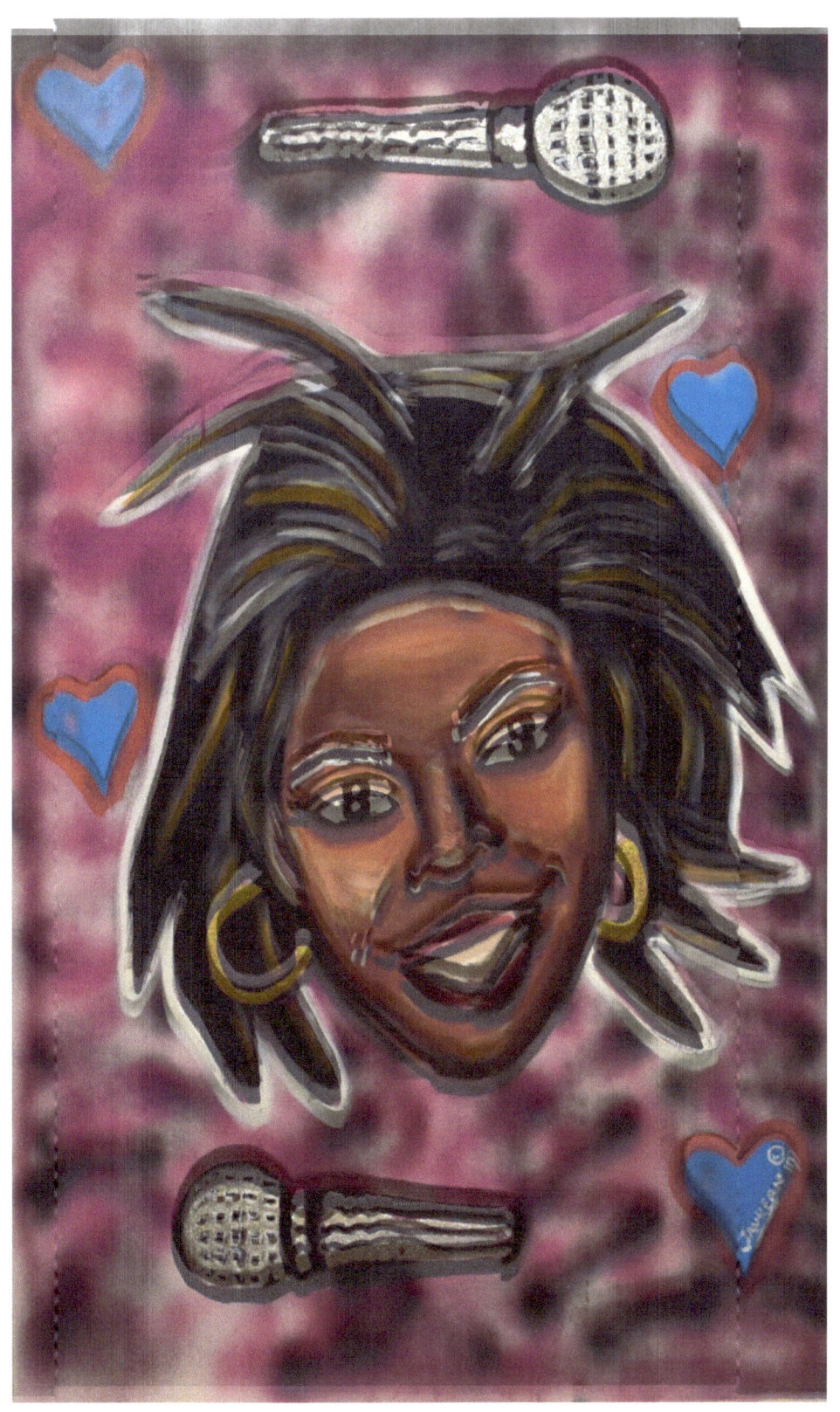

Lauryn Hill (2019)

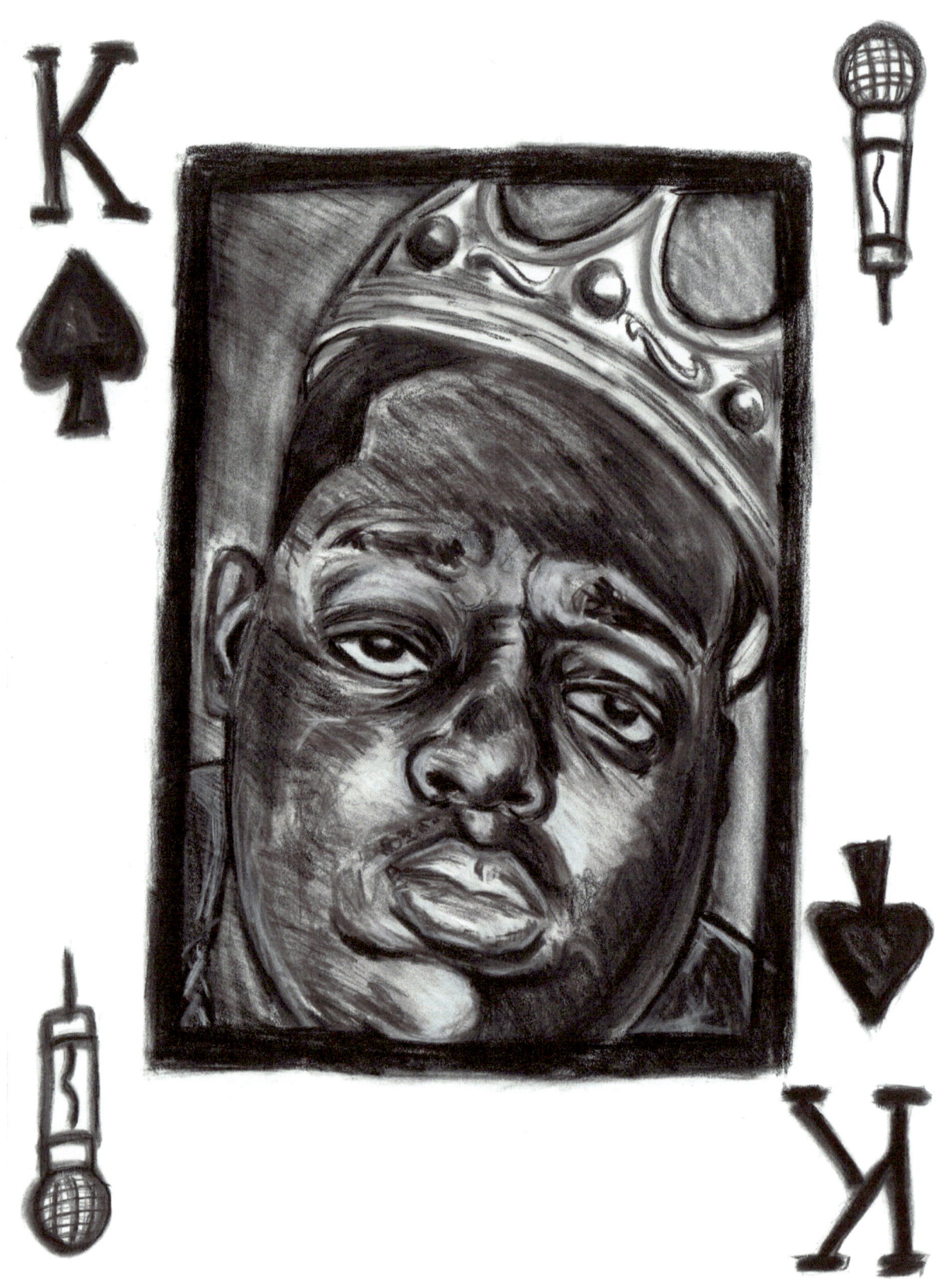

Notorious B.I.G. (2011) RIP

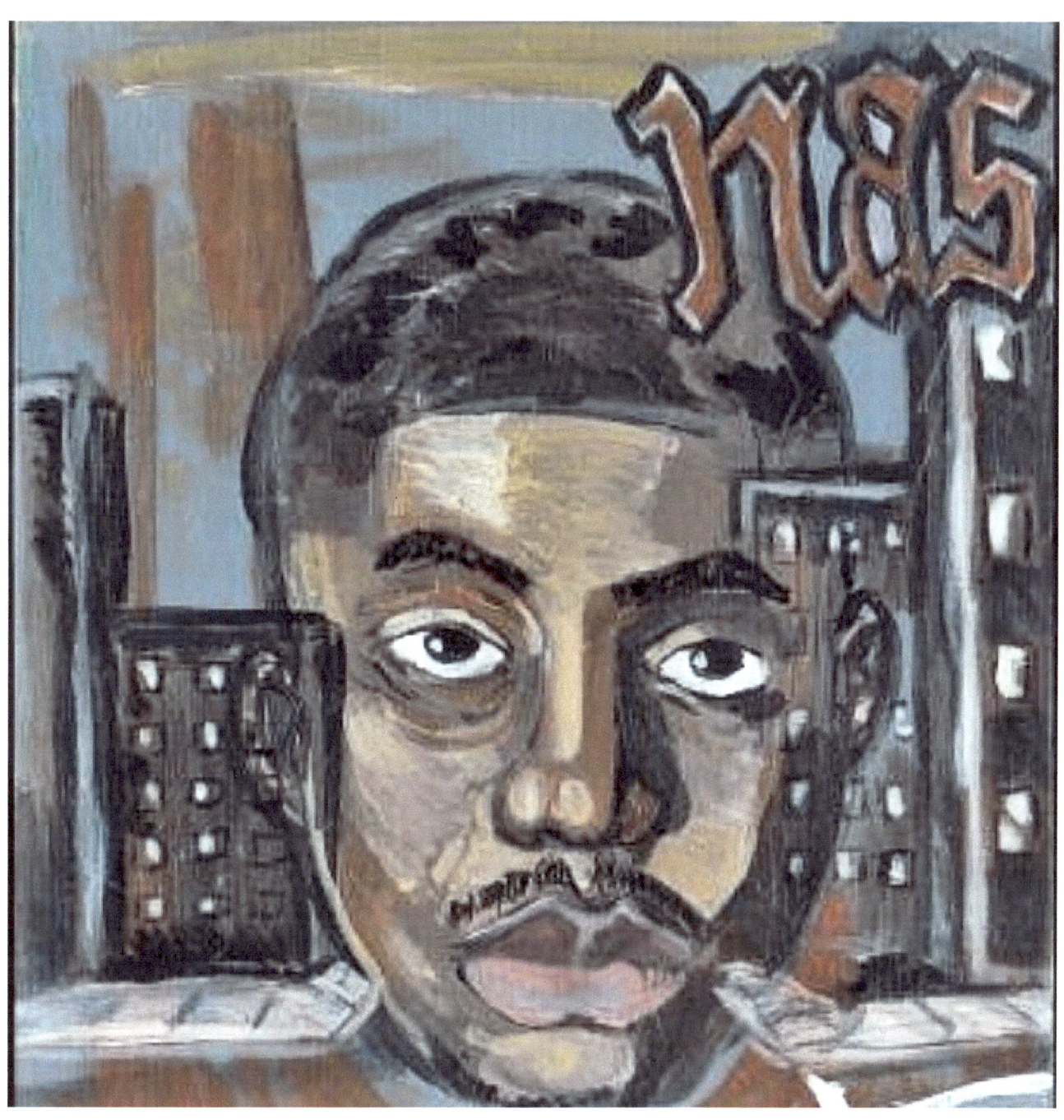

Nas (2011)

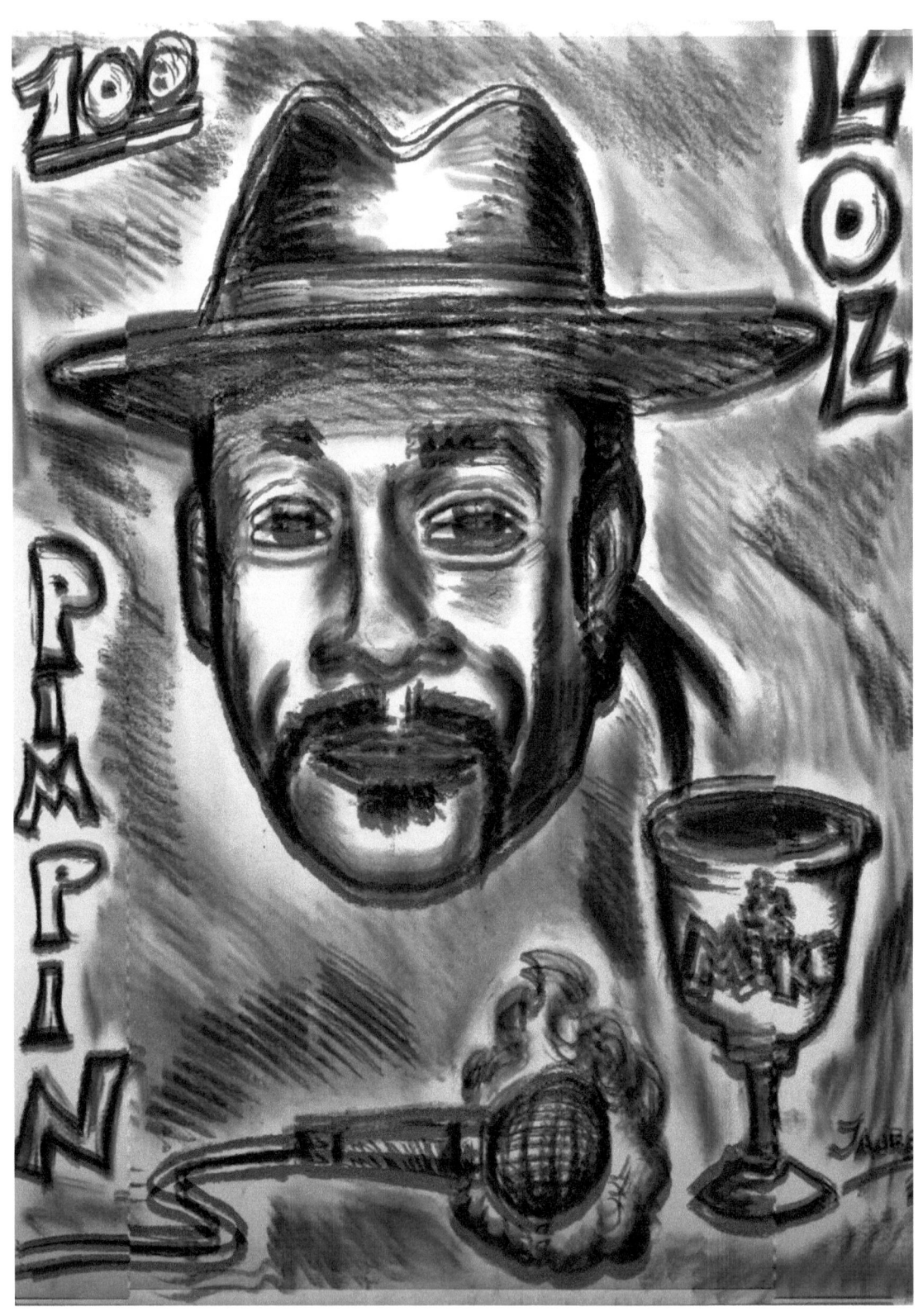

Katt Williams (2023)

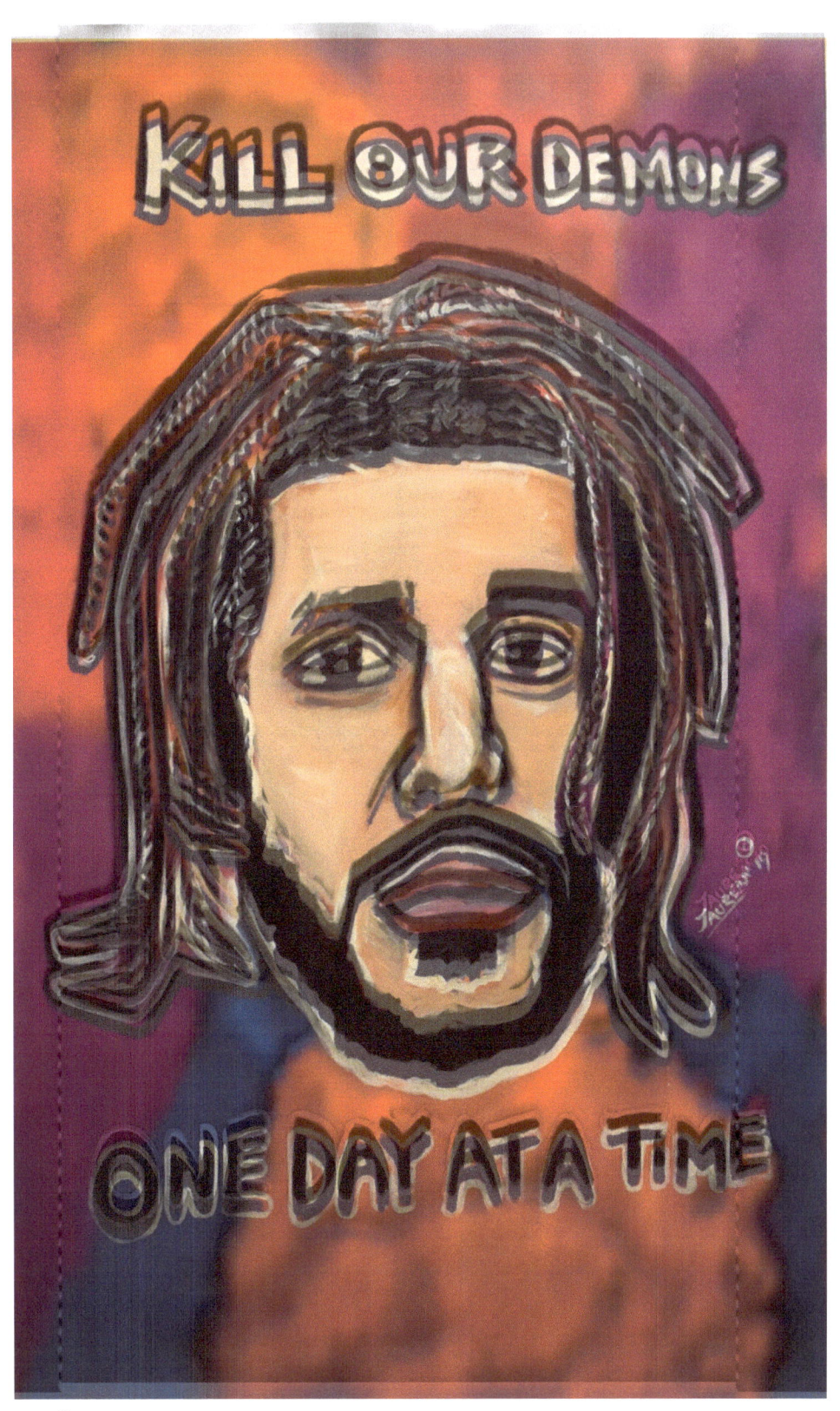

J.Cole (2019)

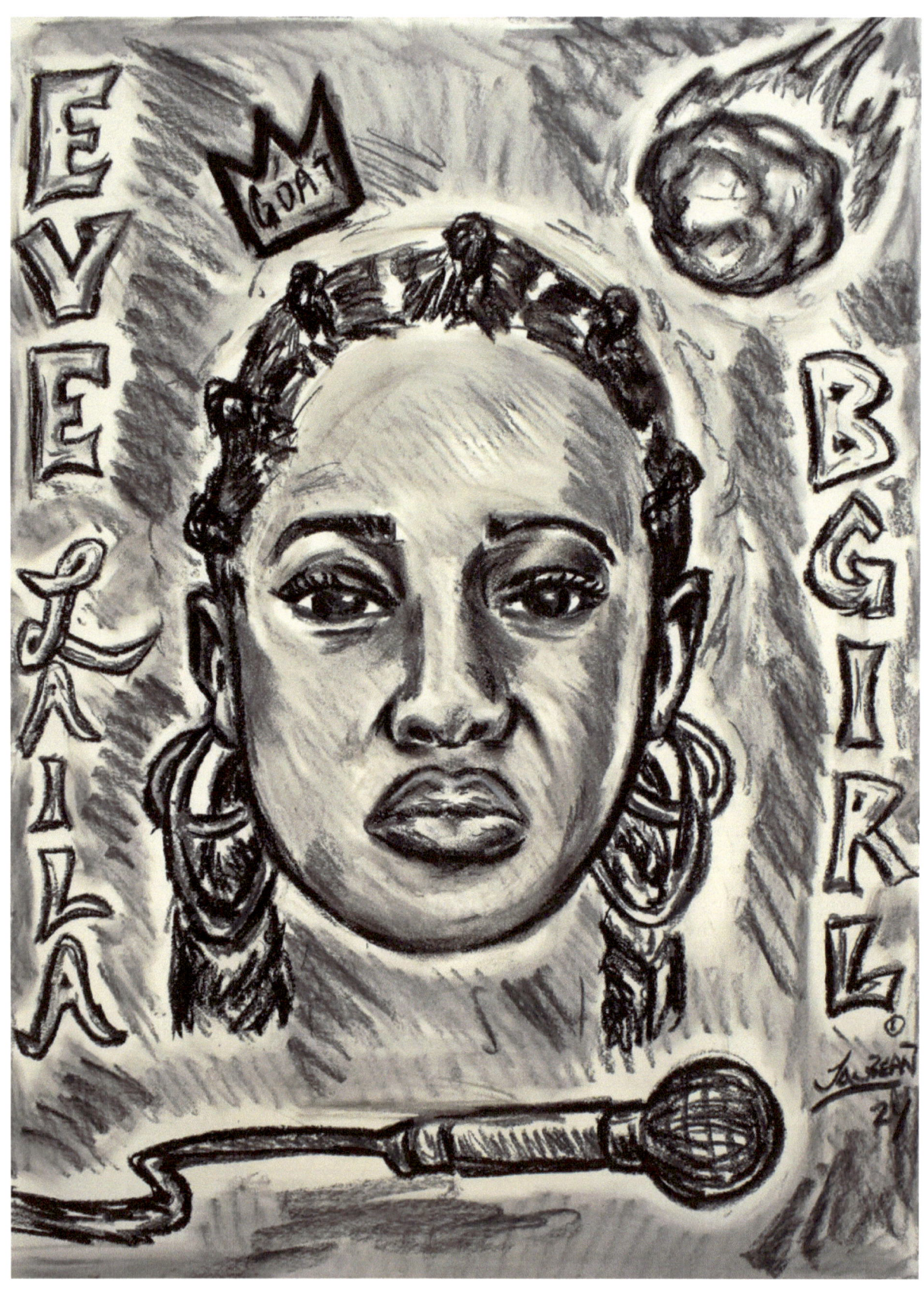

Rapsody (2023)

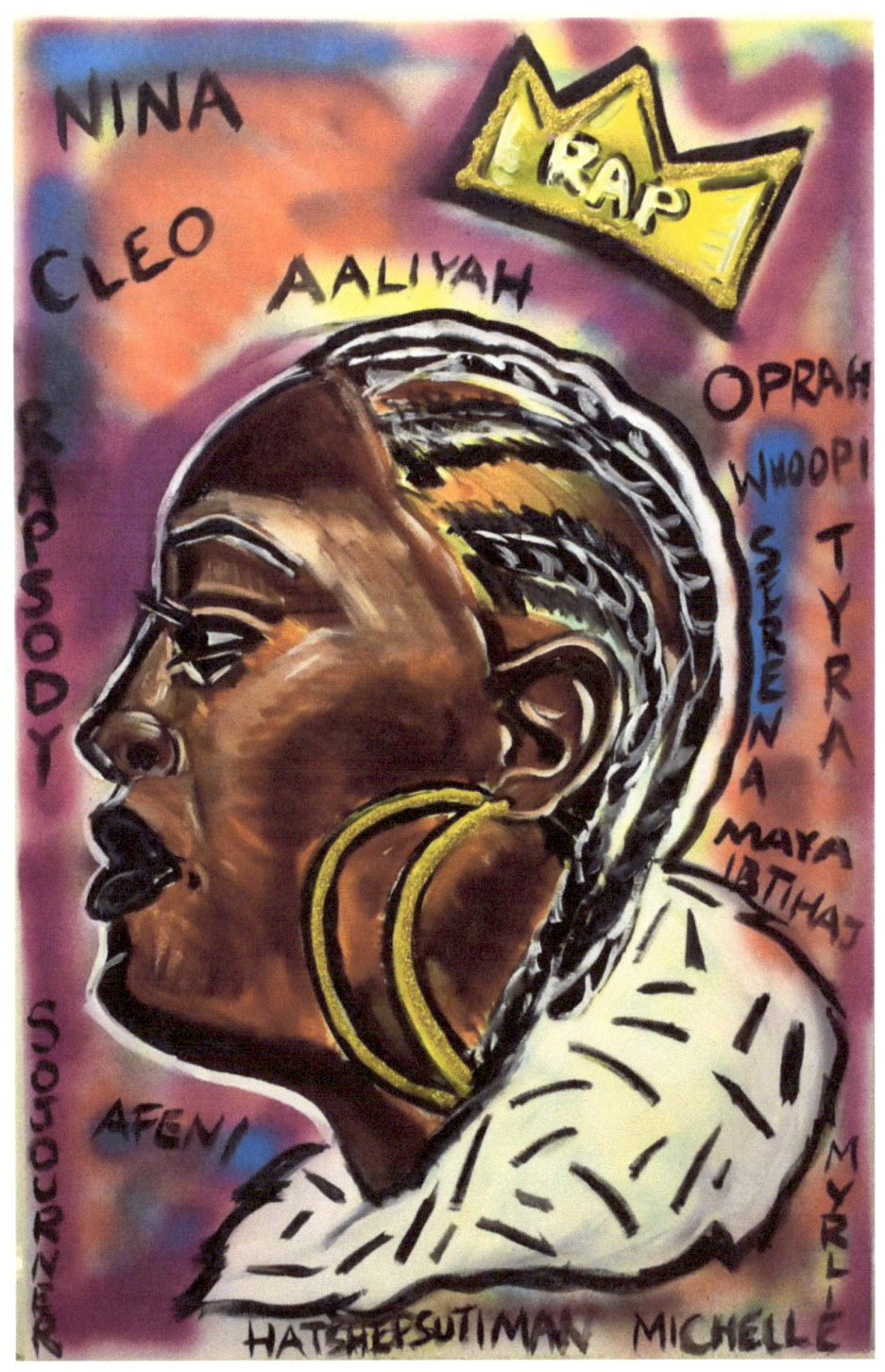

Rapsody (2019)

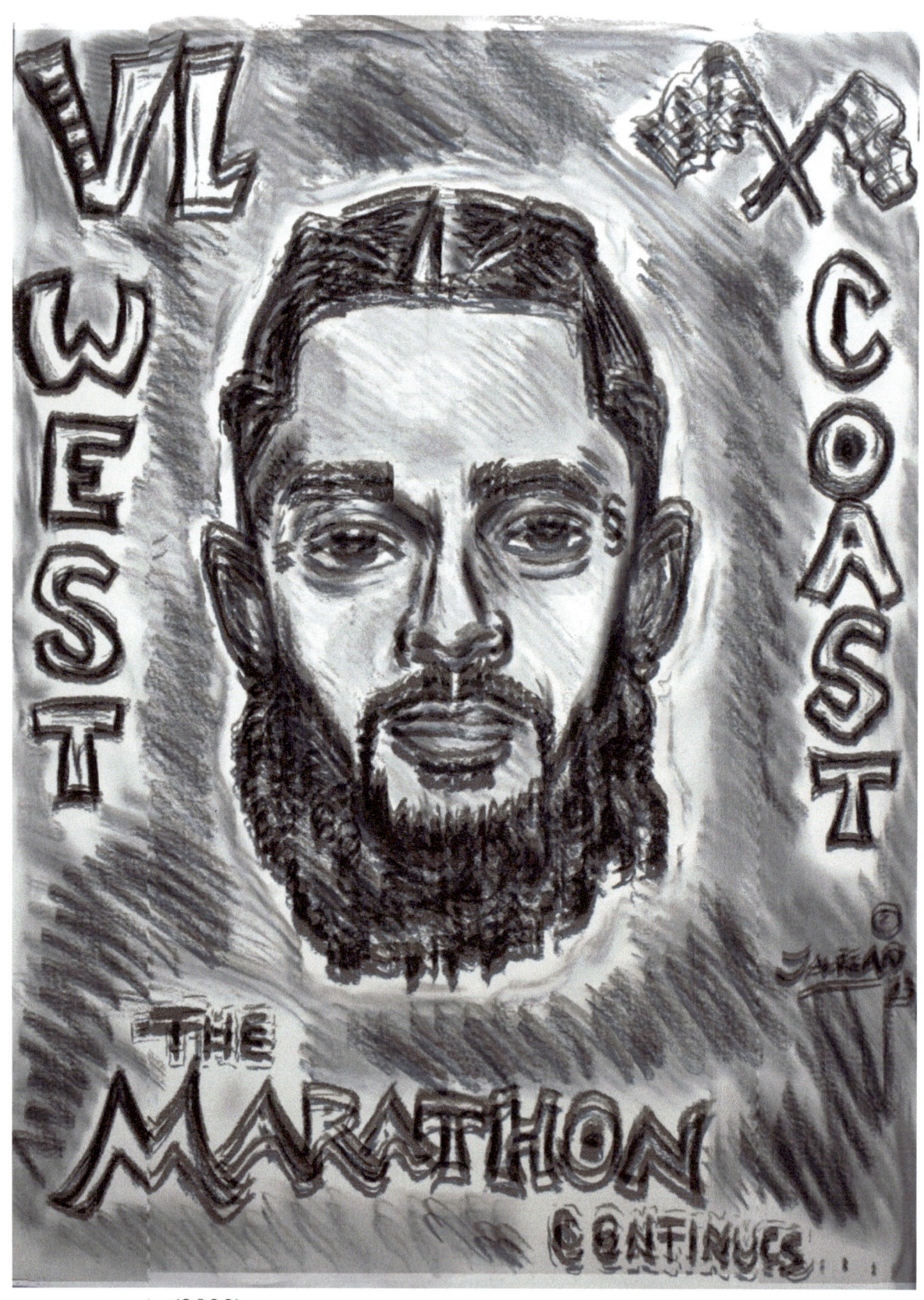

Nipsey Hussle (2023) RIP

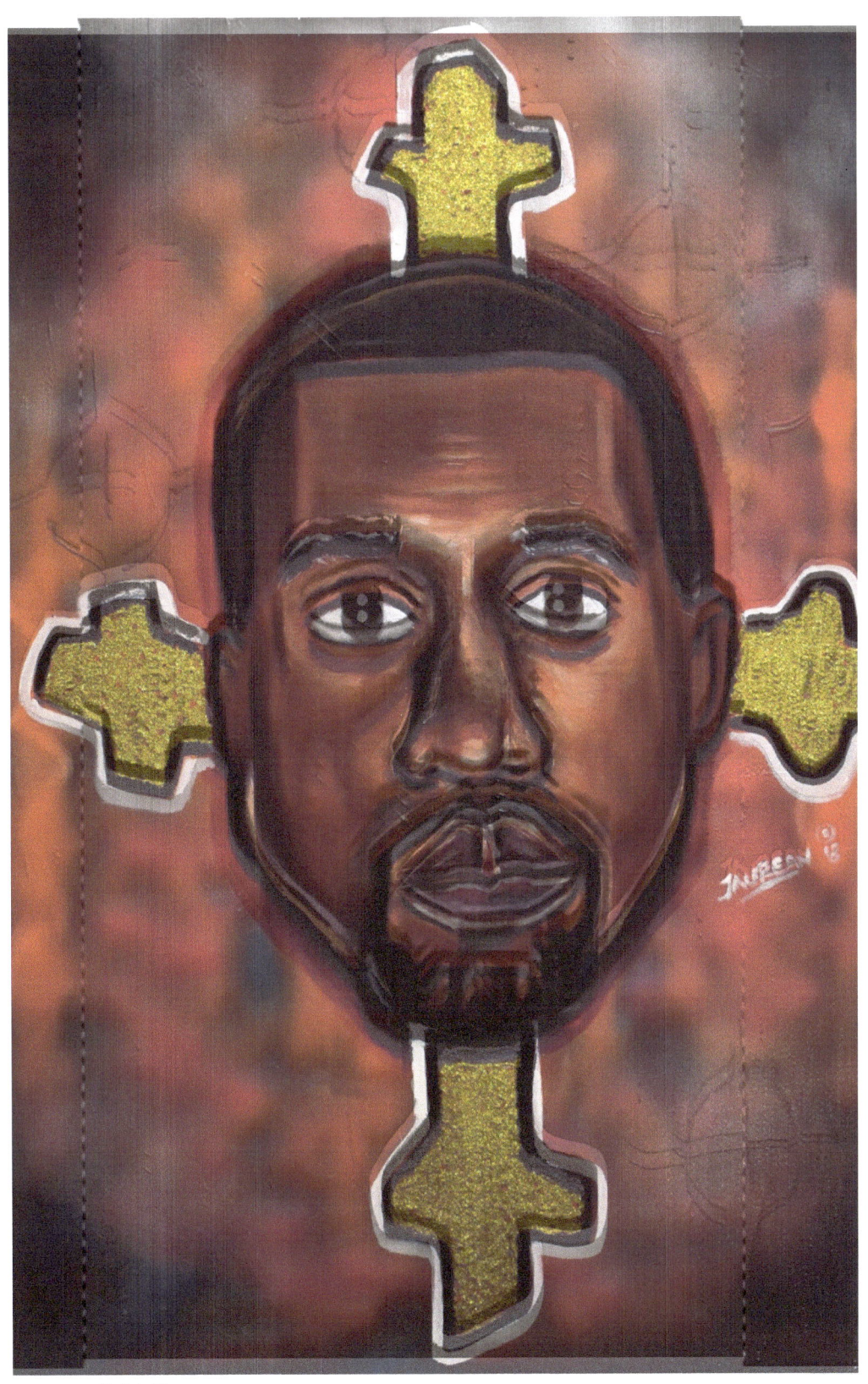

Kanye West (2018)

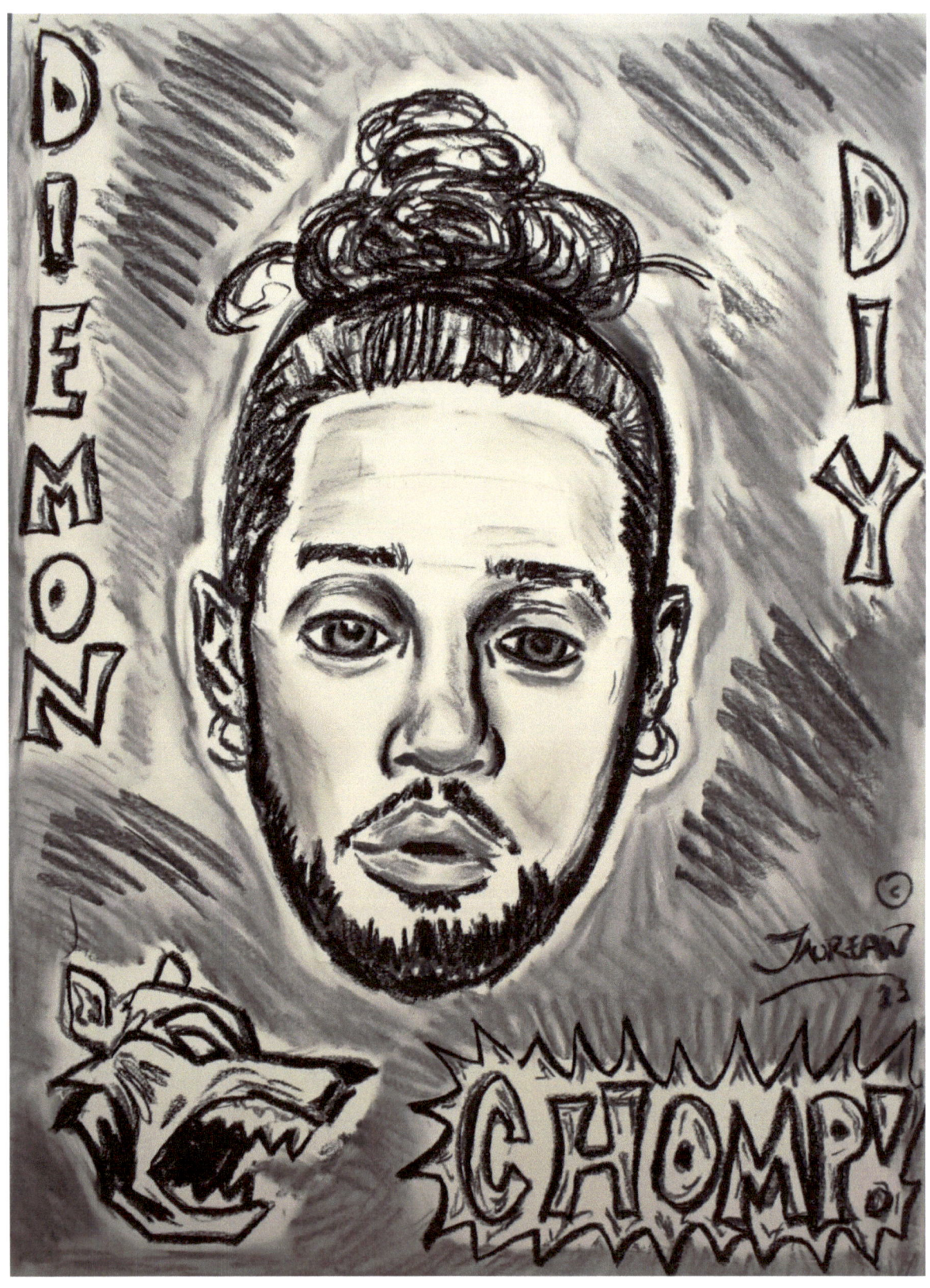

Russ (2023)

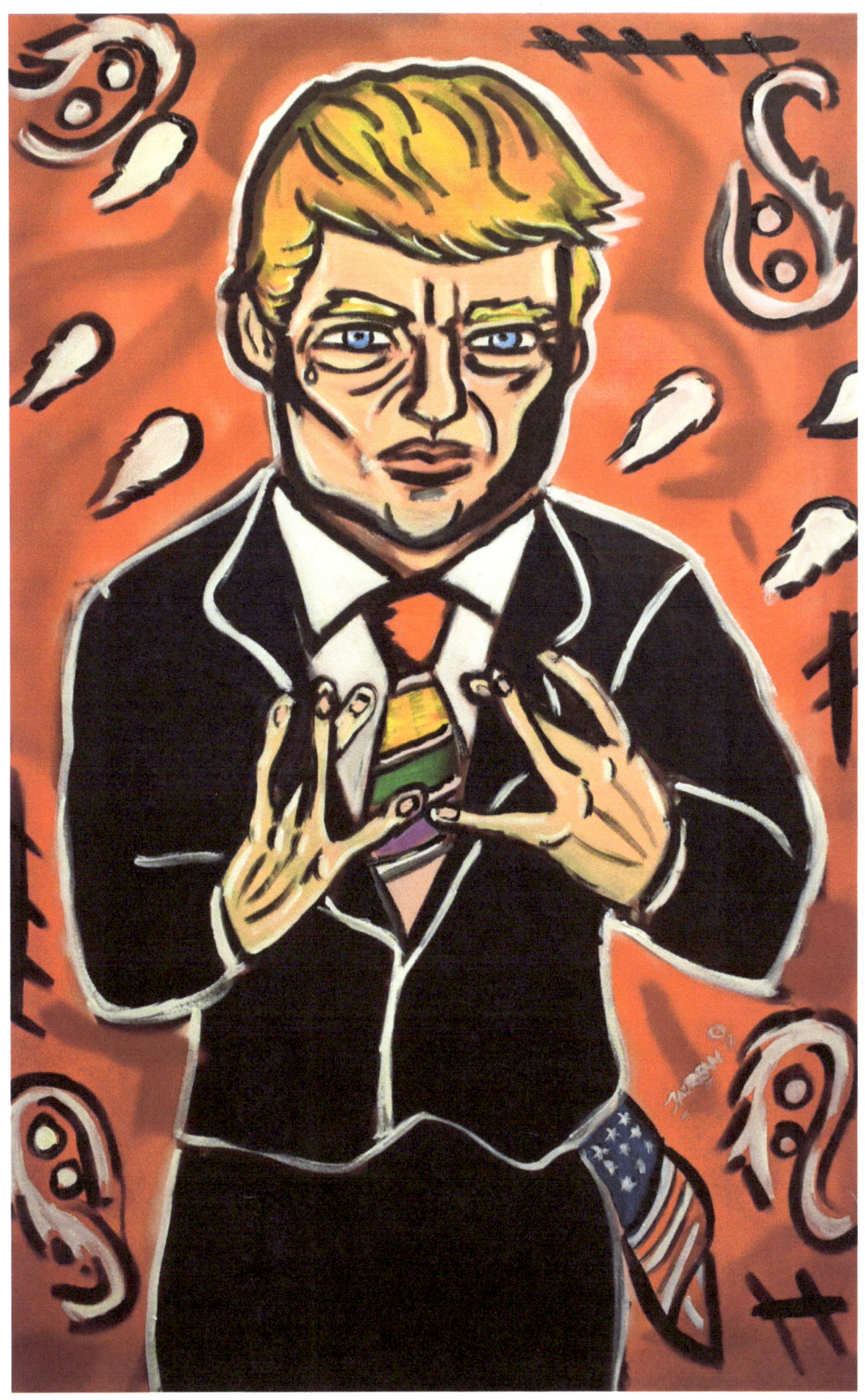

Donald Trump (2018)

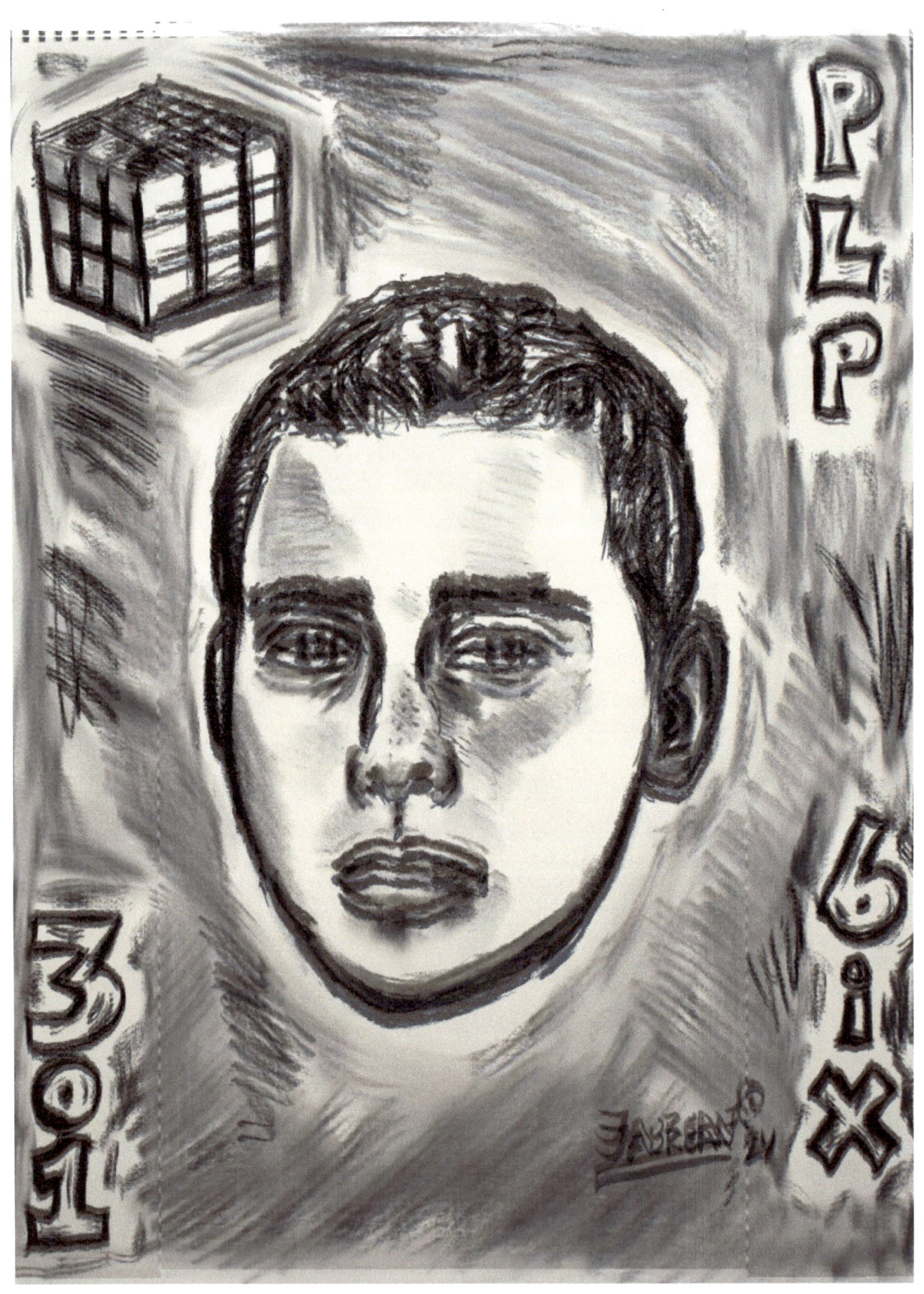

Logic (2024) DMV Stand UP!

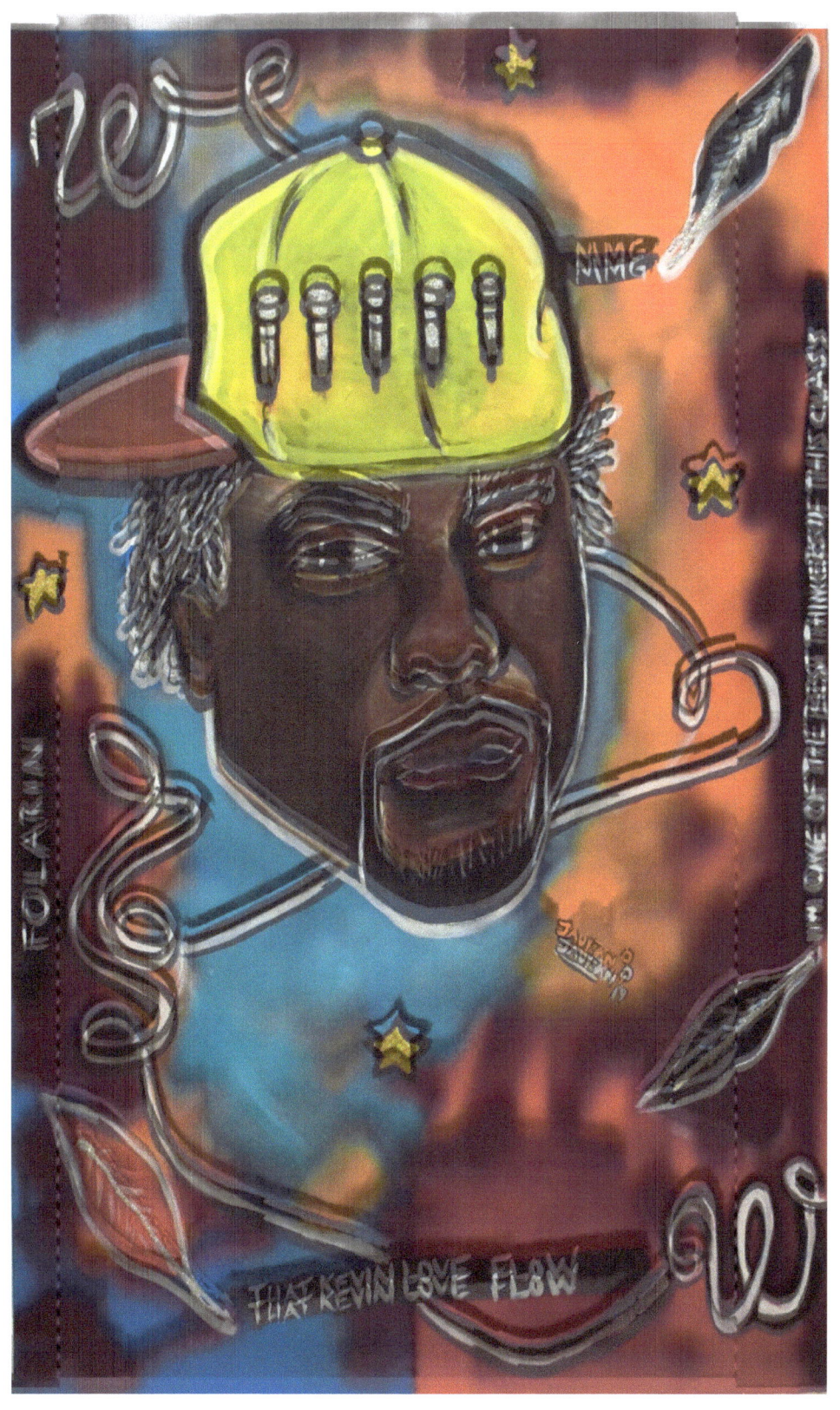

Wale (2019) DMV Stand Up!

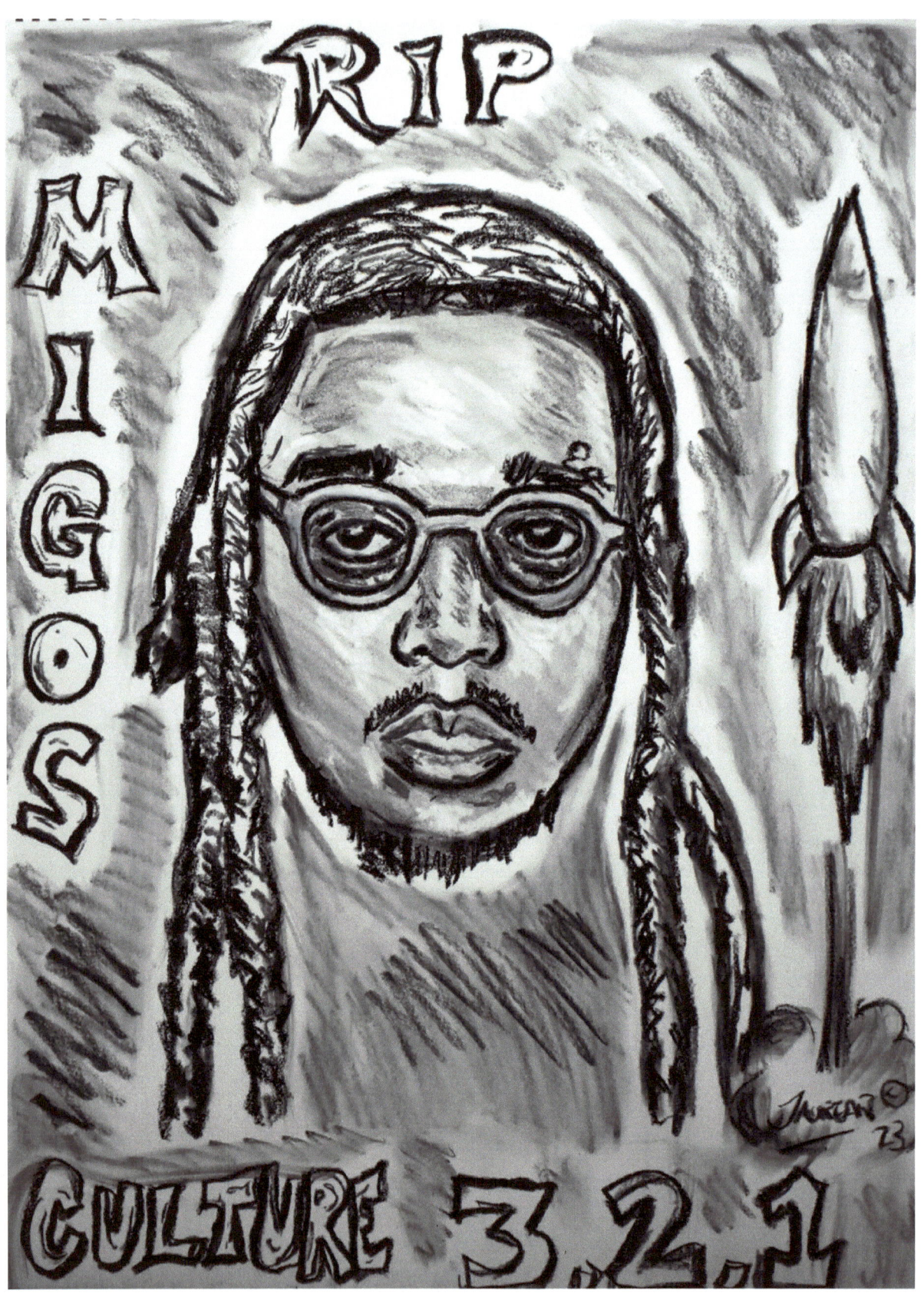

Takeoff (2023) RIP

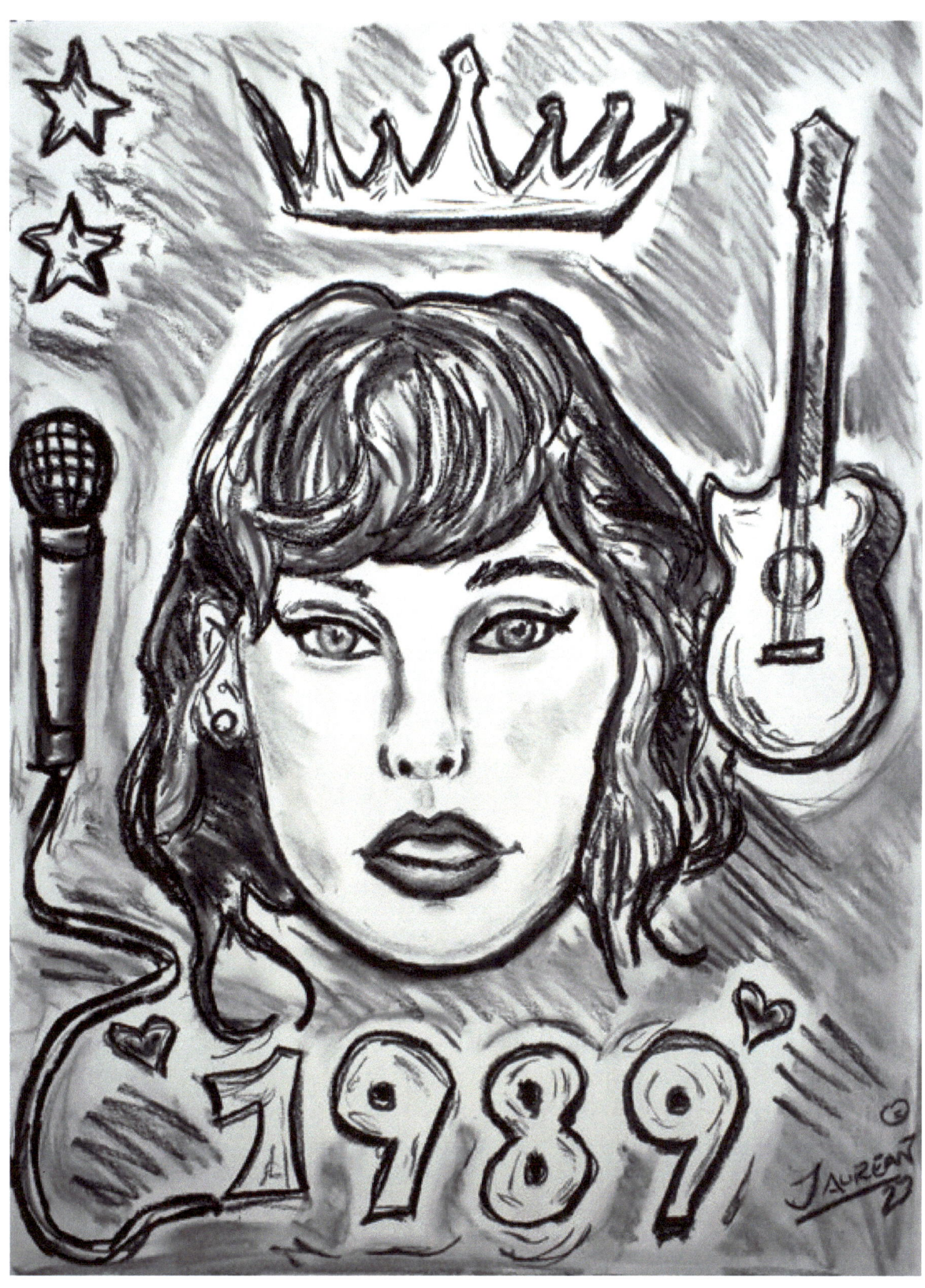

Taylor Swift (2023)

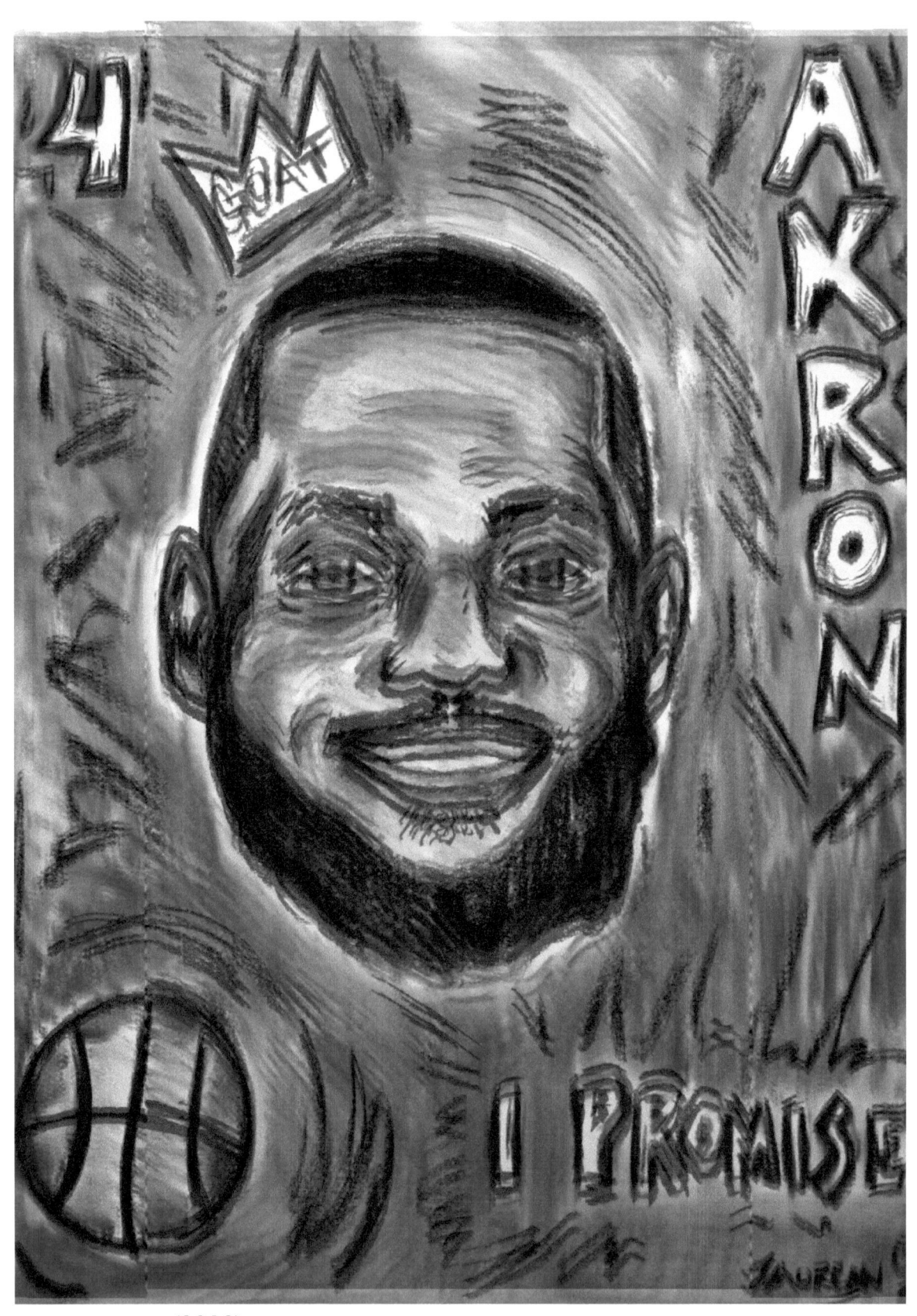

Lebron James (2023)

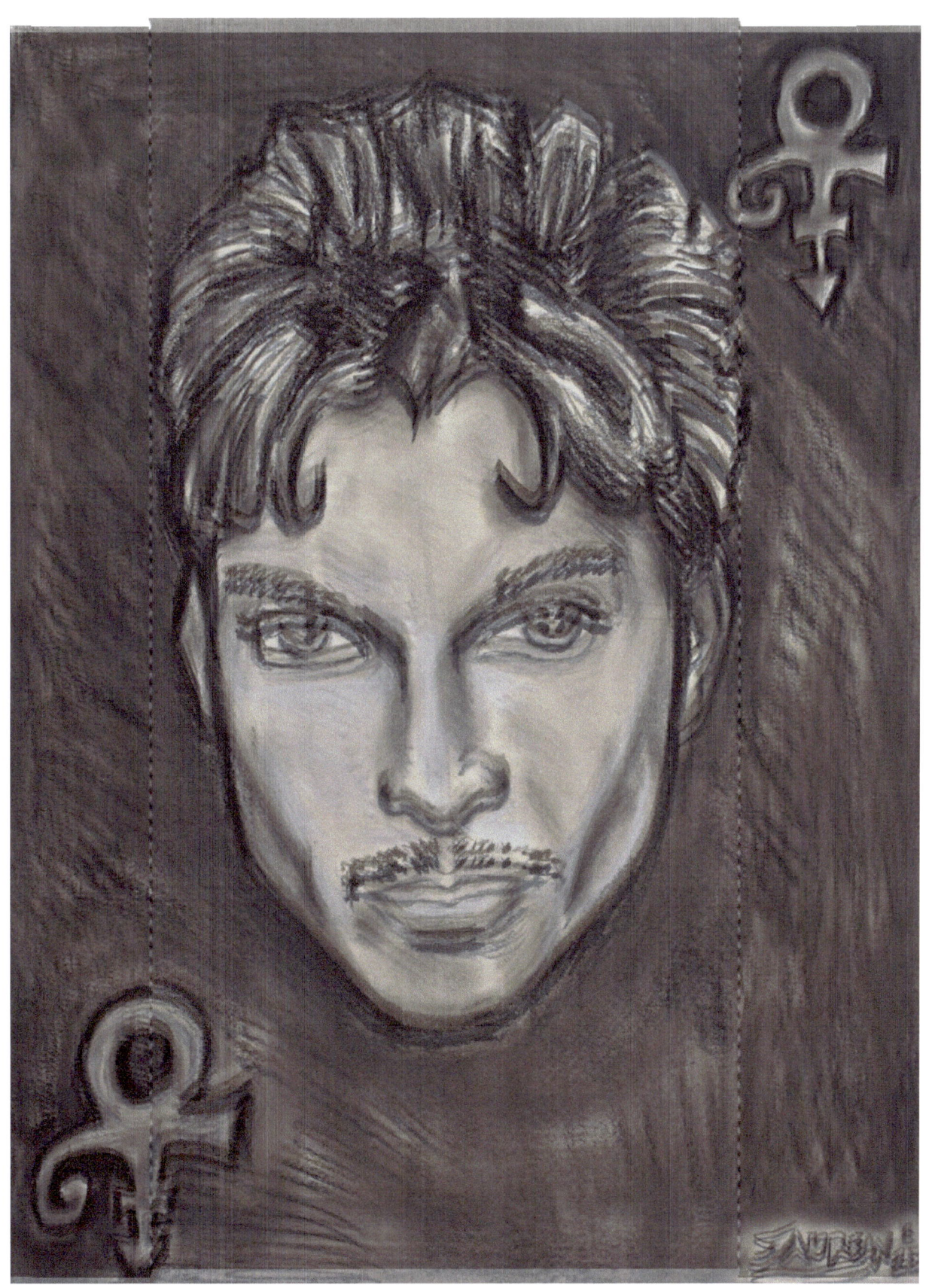

Prince (2023) Rest in Peace

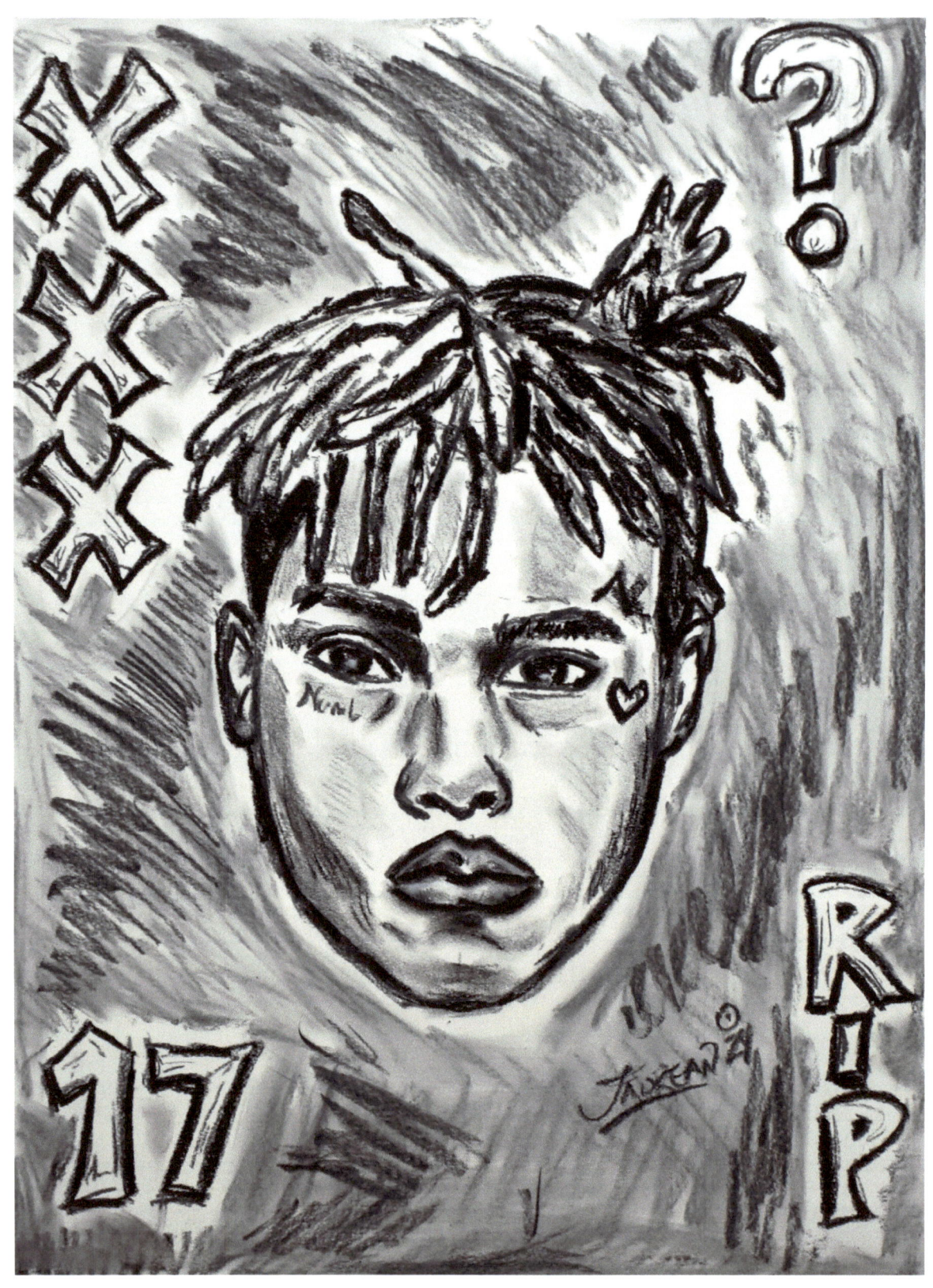

XXXTentacion (2024) RIP

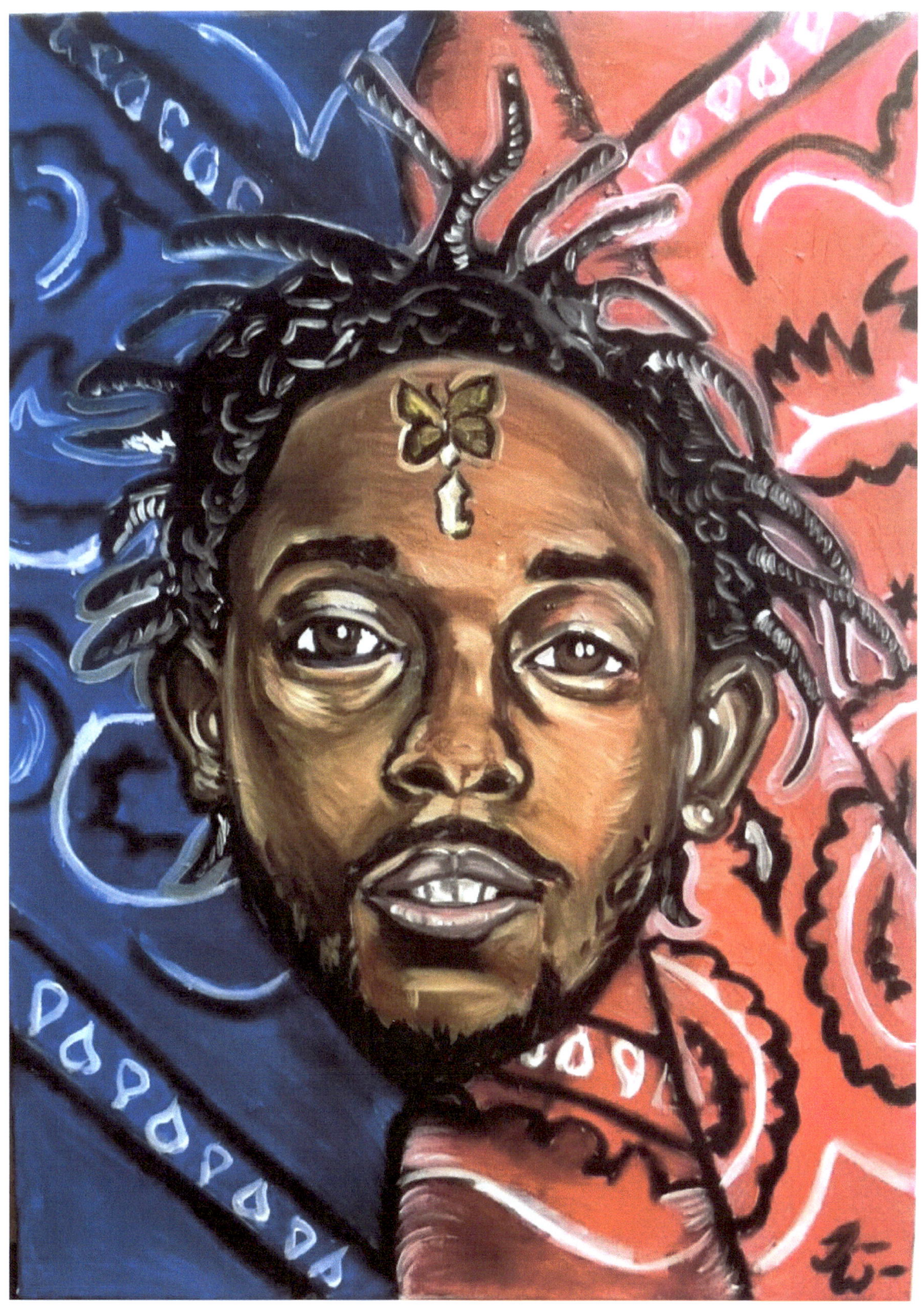

Kendrick Lamar (2015)

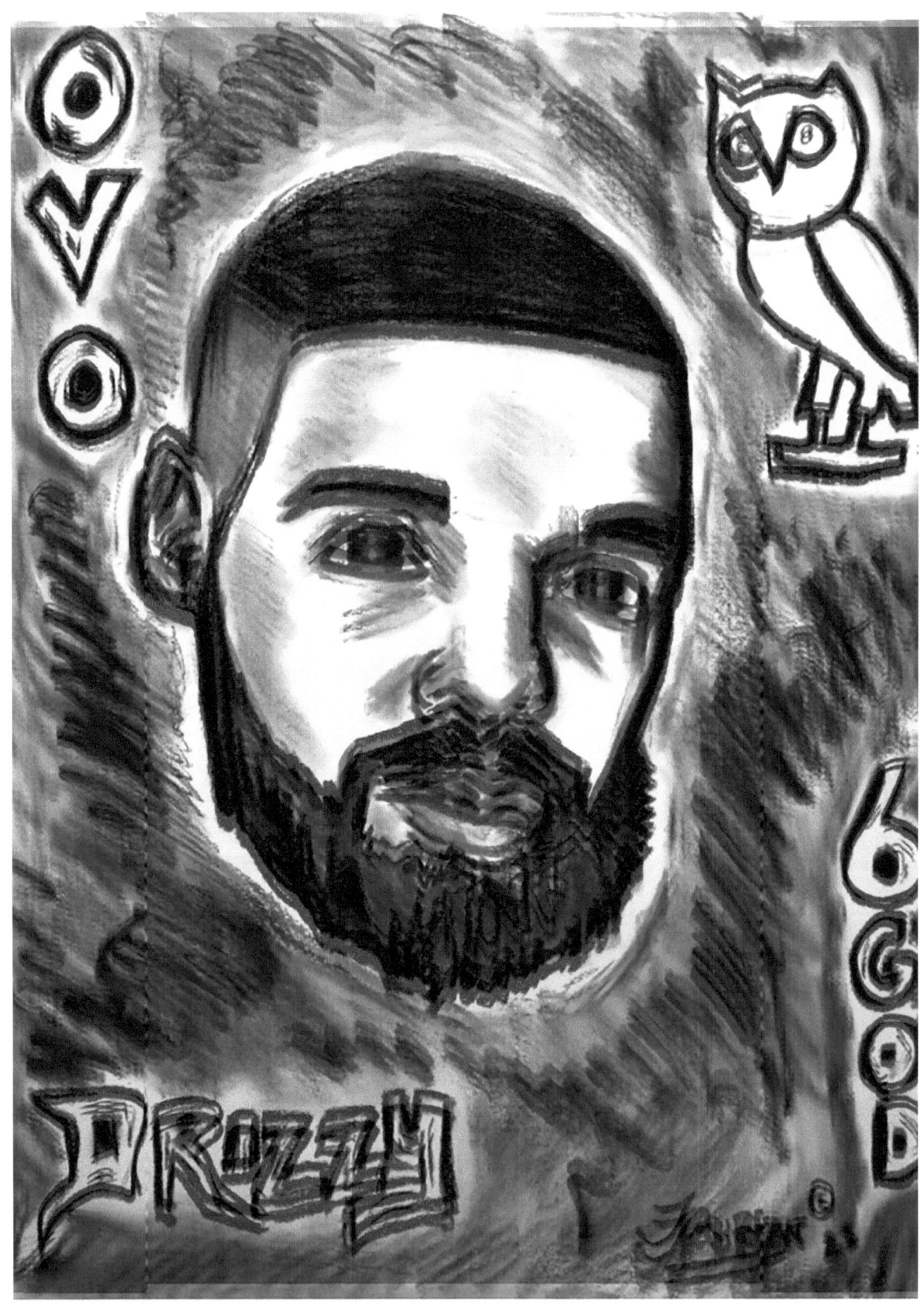

Drake (2023)

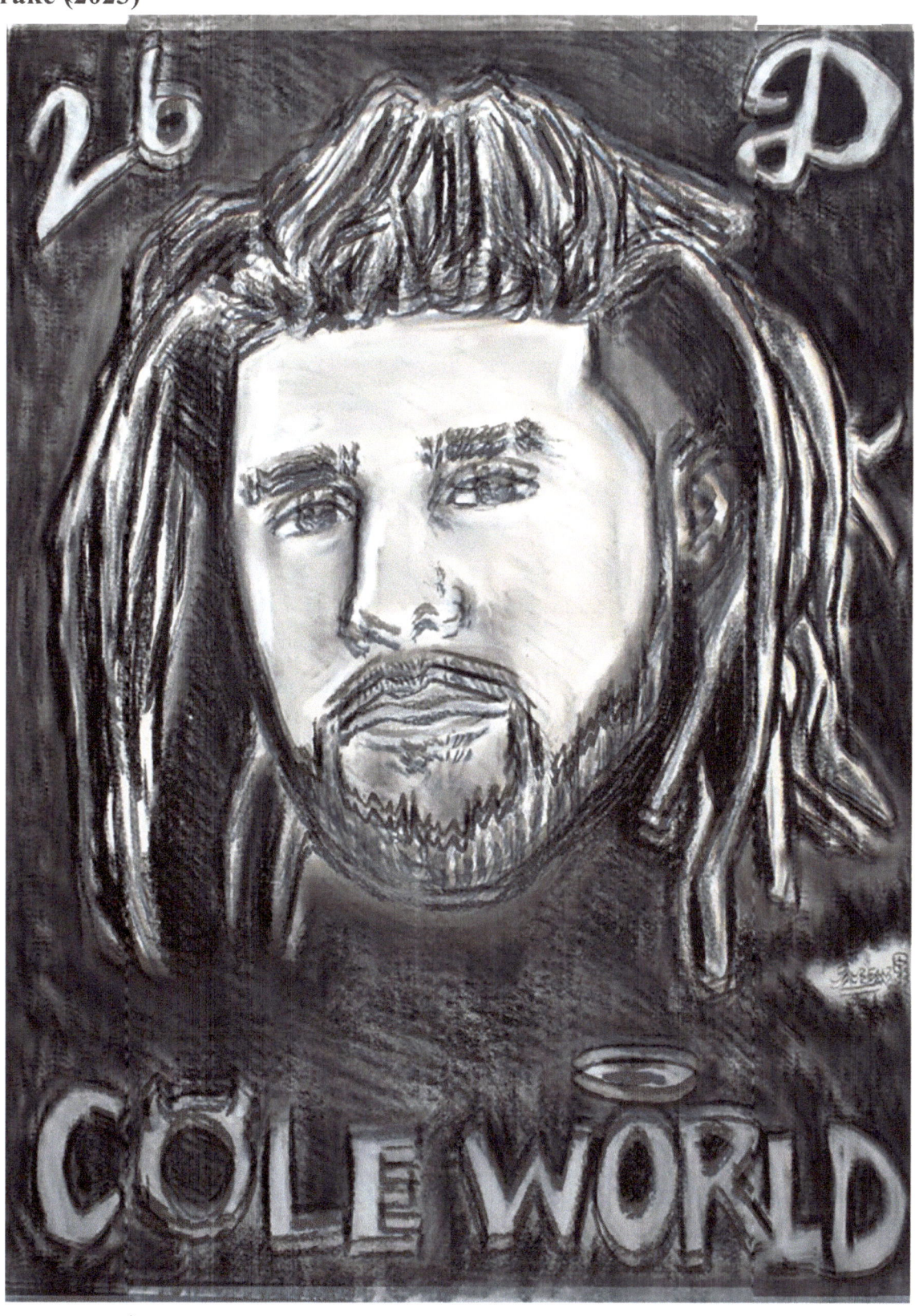

J.Cole (2023)

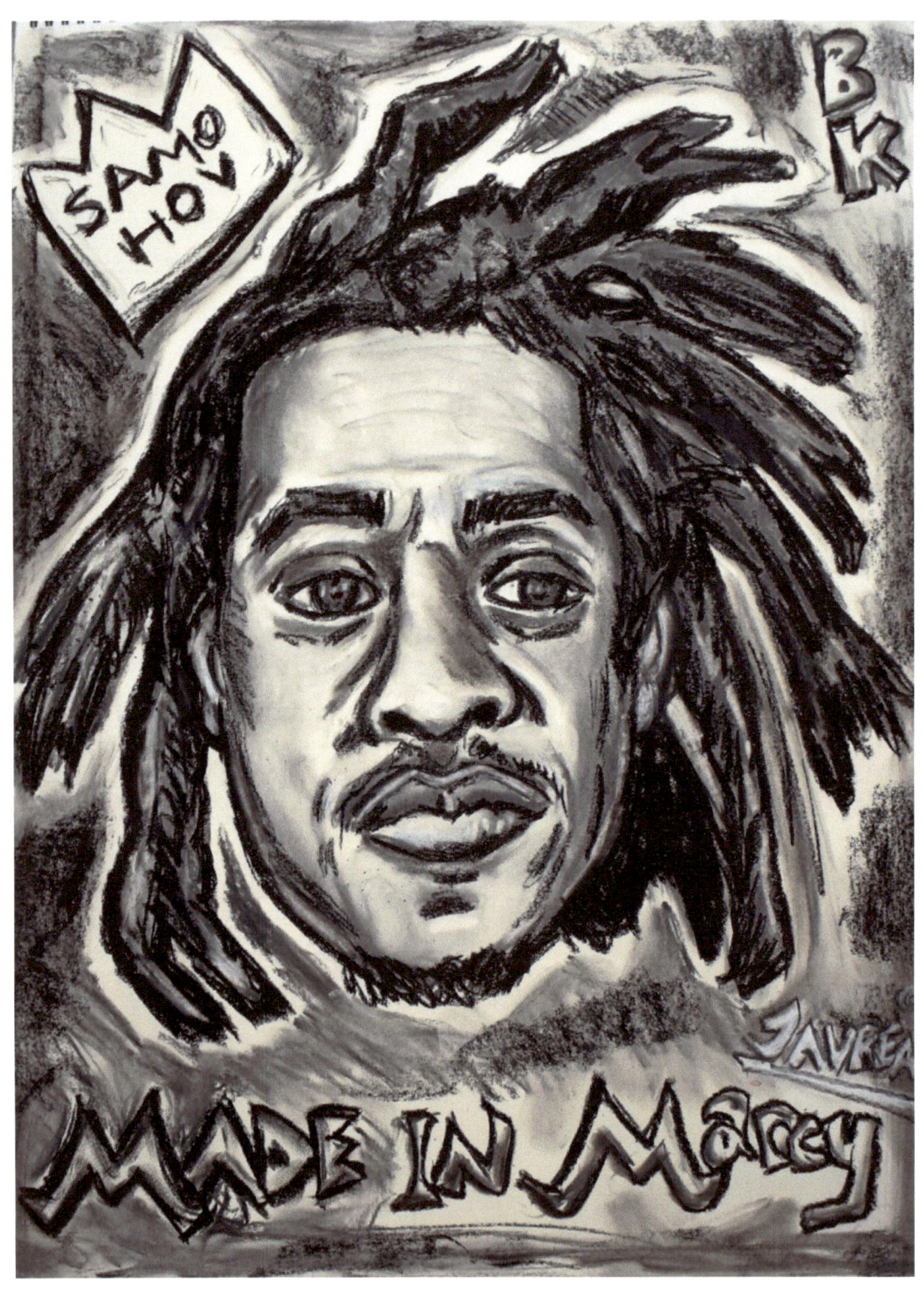

Jay-Z (2024)

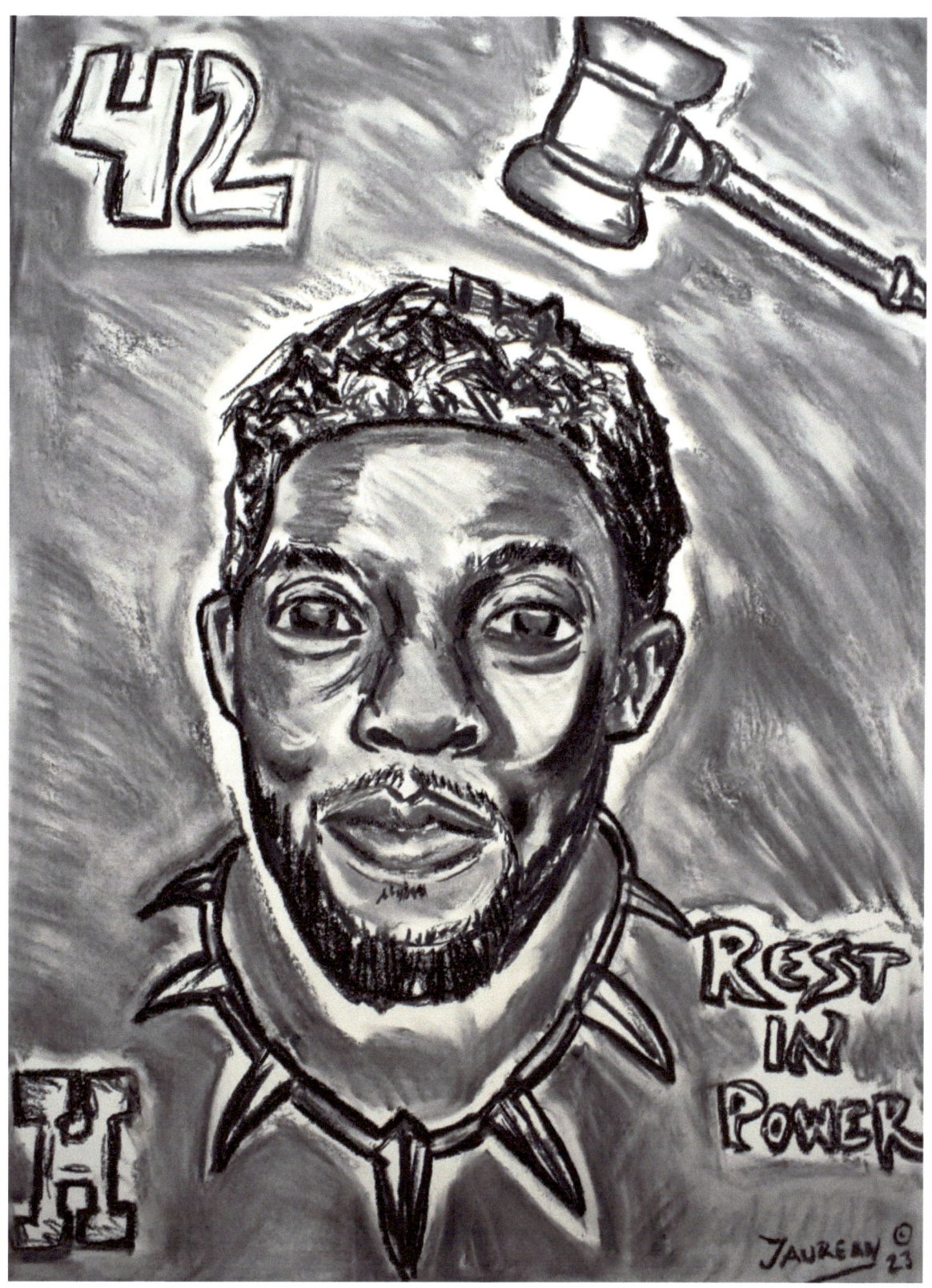

Chadwick Boseman (2023) Rest in Peace King!